BUILDING GREAT SOFTWARE ENGINEERING TEAMS

RECRUITING, HIRING, AND MANAGING YOUR TEAM FROM STARTUP TO SUCCESS

Josh Tyler

Apress®

Building Great Software Engineering Teams: Recruiting, Hiring, and Managing Your Team from Startup to Success

ISBN-13 (pbk): 978-1-4842-1134-2

ISBN-13 (electronic): 978-1-4842-1133-5

Managing Director: Welmoed Spahr
Acquisitions Editor: Robert Hutchinson
Developmental Editor: Douglas Pundick
Editorial Board: Steve Anglin, Mark Beckner, Gary Cornell, Louise Corrigan, James DeWolf, Jonathan Gennick, Robert Hutchinson, Celestin Suresh John, Michelle Lowman, James Markham, Susan McDermott, Matthew Moodie, Jeffrey Pepper, Douglas Pundick, Ben Renow-Clarke, Gwenan Spearing, Matt Wade, Steve Weiss
Coordinating Editor: Rita Fernando
Copy Editors: Kezia Endsley, Sharon Wilkey
Compositor: SPi Global
Indexer: SPi Global
Cover Designer: Friedhelm Steinen-Broo

Distributed to the book trade worldwide by Springer Science+Business Media New York, 233 Spring Street, 6th Floor, New York, NY 10013. Phone 1-800-SPRINGER, fax (201) 348-4505, e-mail orders-ny@springer-sbm.com, or visit www.springeronline.com. Apress Media LLC is a California LLC and the sole member (owner) is Springer Science+Business Media Finance Inc. (SSBM Finance Inc.). SSBM Finance Inc. is a Delaware corporation.

For information on translations, please e-mail rights@apress.com, or visit www.apress.com.

Apress and friends of ED books may be purchased in bulk for academic, corporate, or promotional use. eBook versions and licenses are also available for most titles. For more information, reference our Special Bulk Sales–eBook Licensing web page at www.apress.com/bulk-sales.

Any source code or other supplementary materials referenced by the author in this text is available to readers at www.apress.com. For detailed information about how to locate your book's source code, go to www.apress.com/source-code/.

Apress Business: The Unbiased Source of Business Information

Apress business books provide essential information and practical advice, each written for practitioners by recognized experts. Busy managers and professionals in all areas of the business world—and at all levels of technical sophistication—look to our books for the actionable ideas and tools they need to solve problems, update and enhance their professional skills, make their work lives easier, and capitalize on opportunity.

Whatever the topic on the business spectrum—entrepreneurship, finance, sales, marketing, management, regulation, information technology, among others—Apress has been praised for providing the objective information and unbiased advice you need to excel in your daily work life. Our authors have no axes to grind; they understand they have one job only—to deliver up-to-date, accurate information simply, concisely, and with deep insight that addresses the real needs of our readers.

It is increasingly hard to find information—whether in the news media, on the Internet, and now all too often in books—that is even-handed and has your best interests at heart. We therefore hope that you enjoy this book, which has been carefully crafted to meet our standards of quality and unbiased coverage.

We are always interested in your feedback or ideas for new titles. Perhaps you'd even like to write a book yourself. Whatever the case, reach out to us at editorial@apress.com and an editor will respond swiftly. Incidentally, at the back of this book, you will find a list of useful related titles. Please visit us at www.apress.com to sign up for newsletters and discounts on future purchases.

The Apress Business Team

To my teams—past, present, and future

Contents

About the Author

Josh Tyler is vice president of engineering and design at Course Hero, an education technology company. He was previously director of software engineering at Suitable Technologies and worked in the field of human-computer interaction as a user experience architect, software developer, and researcher at Willow Garage, Zvents, Hewlett-Packard, and Xerox PARC. Tyler holds a BS in computer science from Washington University and an MS in computer science from Stanford University.

Acknowledgments

So many people have helped me get where I am today that I don't know where to begin.

Actually, I do. Angelina Calderon, our lead recruiter at The Sourcery, has been so much more than I expected when we began working together. Her ideas, feedback, and intuition have shaped a lot of what you see in this book. Thank you so much, Angelina and team.

There are many other people I wish to thank as well: Andrew Grauer, CEO of Course Hero, for giving me the opportunity and support to build a great team; the rest of the team at Course Hero, especially the senior engineers, for the parts you play in our process; Scott Hassan, who gave me a unique opportunity to lead development on some really cool robots; Robert Krohn, for giving me my first crack at management; Steve Cousins, for mentorship throughout my career; Kelly Wachs, for patiently explaining many details of employment-based immigration law; James A. Bach, author of *How to Secure Your H-1B Visa*, for his help reviewing my writing; my old friends Gordon Rios, Ethan Stock, Stephen Sorkin, Jeff Gray, and Cole Goeppinger, to whom I turn when I have management challenges; Dionne McCray, for her tough love and pushing me to be more than I thought I could; and Amit Nithianandan, for reviewing my writing along the way.

From Apress, I wish to thank Robert Hutchinson, for believing in me from the beginning; Rita Fernando, for helping me through the process as a first-time author; and Douglas Pundick, for cleaning up all my prose.

And finally, I wish to thank my family—my wonderful and brilliant wife, Gesara, who continues to be my most trusted advisor on all matters, professional and personal; my kids, for having the patience to let me finish this project; my parents, for their support and encouragement; and everyone else in my family, just for being who they are.

Thanks, everyone.

Introduction

In my career as a software engineer, manager, and executive, I've read many great books and other resources on the challenges of finding and managing software engineers. I have never found, however, a comprehensive guide for a specific problem that I've faced several times: getting a startup engineering team off the ground.

Over the years, I've gradually created and refined a set of thoughts on this topic. With this book, I aim to provide a thorough guide to the most important challenges of building and managing a software team in a competitive, fast-paced environment.

Who Should Read This Book?

This book will be useful for anyone trying to hire software engineers. More specifically, however, it's targeted at people in the following roles:

- Startup founders (technical and nontechnical)
- CTOs of startups or small, growing companies
- Engineering managers in fast-growing teams
- Anyone looking to build the skills necessary to succeed in one of the preceding roles

In these high-stakes environments, the challenge of scaling up an engineering team can be intimidating. Engineering leaders need to know how to find great candidates, create effective interviewing and hiring processes, bring out the best in their people and their work, provide meaningful career development, learn to spot warning signs in their team, and manage people for long-term success.

What Will You Learn?

In this book, you'll learn how to build your software team, starting with your first hire and continuing through the stages of development you'll encounter as you manage your team for growth and success. Designed to cover each step of the process in the order you'll likely face them, and highlighted by stories of success and failure, this book provides an easy-to-understand recipe for creating your high-powered engineering team.

Here are some specific topics we'll cover:

- Effective techniques for finding engineering candidates for your company, including how to make your company more attractive to prospective employees

- Tips for navigating the employment visa process

- How to leverage commonly overlooked resources for finding employees, such as hiring from other geographic regions

- How to approach college recruiting

- How to successfully hire the best candidates, from first contact through making an offer and getting it accepted

- How to manage engineers for optimal morale and performance, foster confidence throughout your organization, and promote career development for your team members

- What to expect as you build an engineering team: common challenges, growing pains, and solutions

- How to use team-building skills to propel your career as an individual contributor

This book is organized into three parts: Recruiting, Hiring, and Managing, followed by an appendix of useful advice for anyone in a software engineering career. You don't need to read it from front to back—feel free to skip to any section that covers a topic of the most interest to you, or an issue you're currently facing.

I sincerely hope and believe this book will help many aspiring founders, managers, and team-builders unlock the growth potential present in their teams.

The Challenge of Building an Engineering Team

Startups fall into one of two groups: Growing and Dying.

There's no in-between.

To clarify, in this book the term *startup* refers to a product-oriented company in the process of finding and scaling a high-growth business model. There are many kinds of small, young, and growing companies, but this book focuses on the experience of technology startups, most likely backed by venture capital or seed funding, of the sort you find in Silicon Valley and other major tech hubs.

If your company is growing, odds are good that you're looking to hire software engineers. You know that hiring engineers is difficult, either from personal experience or because everyone tells you so.

The purpose of this book is to show you how to make tangible progress on this intimidating problem. Though written from the perspective of a startup, the material here should be useful for those building technical teams in a variety of environments.

Why Is It So Hard to Build an Engineering Team?

Building an engineering team is a multidimensional challenge. The high-risk, high-reward nature of technology startups means that some will be huge successes, but only very few. The economics of venture capital place a huge importance on getting the absolute best talent, especially when it comes to engineers, who are typically the primary builders of a startup's product. Industry conventional wisdom compounds this problem by promoting the premise that some programmers are 10 times (or even 100 times) more valuable than the "average" coder. It's also difficult to know how to identify top engineers without extensive hands-on experience, which is of course impossible to get in typical interviews.

Once you've finally found an engineer you think is good, getting that person to join your team is another daunting challenge. You're probably competing against other attractive companies and facing unanswerable questions, such as these: How much should we offer? Should we extend our offer deadline? What are the candidate's true decision-making criteria? And so on.

Finally, as you start to assemble a team of promising engineers, you confront one of the most neglected and misunderstood functions in tech startup companies: management. How will you help the people on your team be more productive, happy, and grow their own capabilities along with the company?

This book is written for startup founders, engineering managers, and other technical leaders trying to build a team in a high-growth, competitive environment. Before we get into the details of potential techniques, considerations, and solutions for the challenges I've described, let's consider them each in a bit more detail.

Tech Talent Is in Short Supply

The rise of computing technology has created an ever-increasing demand for people who can write the software to control nearly all aspects of our economy and industry. As noted entrepreneur and investor Marc Andreesseen puts it, "Software is eating the world."[1]

Software isn't written for only desktop computers. It's in everything, from toasters, to laptops, to watches, to mainframe computers, to the systems that control all the life-sustaining infrastructure of the modern world. Tesla Motors isn't a car company; it's a software company that makes cars. Implementing the

---

[1]www.wsj.com/articles/SB10001424053111903480904576512250915629460

Affordable Care Act was mostly a software problem (and one that had a few bugs). Google has a team of over 50,000 people to provide search results for one empty text box.

Unfortunately, the world's educational system hasn't produced software engineers to meet the rate of job creation. And it's likely to get worse: "Employment of software developers is projected to grow 22 percent from 2012 to 2022, much faster than the average for all occupations. The main reason for the rapid growth is a large increase in the demand for computer software."[2]

In short, the world needs more programmers.

Tech Culture Exaggerates the Problem

While the engineering shortage is real, it also gets exaggerated in misleading and unproductive ways. Very much a part of tech culture, the difficulty of finding developers is one of the most frequently discussed topics in Silicon Valley—in the media, in coffee shops, and within companies themselves.

While it's easy to simply complain, as many do, that there aren't any engineers available to hire, it's also lazy and not totally accurate. It would be more accurate to say that everyone is trying to hire the same small subset of engineers, and there definitely aren't enough of them to go around.

Why are most companies looking to hire the same people? It starts with the notion of the *10x programmer*—a coder or software engineer who is 10 (or more) times more productive than average. Whether or not you believe this disparity exists, enough people do that competition for possible candidates is fierce.

The problem is that you can't truly and reliably identify 10x talent in your interviews. If you could, engineering salaries would vary by up to 10 times as well. Even at the height of a boom in Silicon Valley, engineers aren't being offered millions per year in salary.

This hasn't stopped some people from trying, however. The ideal candidate typically looks something like this:

- Bachelor's degree in computer science (CS) from Stanford or MIT (advanced degrees are OK but don't really add to perceived value)

- Worked for a little while—but not too long—at a phenomenally successful company (Google or Facebook, for example)

---

[2]www.bls.gov/ooh/computer-and-information-technology/software-developers.htm

- Documented experience with the latest and greatest software development languages, tools, techniques, and frameworks (the specifics depend on the company and market)

The venture capital (VC) industry, which guides so much of what happens in Silicon Valley startups, has a unique approach to maximizing return on investment. VC firms are typically trying to land a small number (even just one) of "homeruns"—deals that make them 100 times, or even 1,000 times the amount they originally put in. For example, in 1999 two firms, Sequoia Capital and Kleiner Perkins Caulfield & Byers, each invested $12.5 million for 10 percent of a fast-growing search startup with a funny name. At the time of this writing, Google's market capitalization is near $400 billion, meaning that, even considering dilution and other factors, each firm's stake would be worth well over 1,000 times the original amount.

This high-stakes, winner-take-all (or close to it) environment further fuels the notion that you must find the absolute best, the elite technical minds of the world, in order to succeed. If you're hoping to see an investment grow by at least 10 times, it's logically consistent to look for 10x staff, including programmers. And since the early-stage startups are mostly programmers, that's the role for which this problem is most acute.

The emphasis on finding premier engineers has permeated the culture and vocabulary of Silicon Valley. It's not enough to hire a good coder—they need to be "rock stars" or "ninjas." Not only is this approach arbitrary and elitist, it's not even accurate.

A great engineer has little in common with a true rock star. Music and entertainment icons must relish the spotlight and play up a larger-than-life persona. It's hard to imagine a successful engineering career with similar behavior. Nor would you want an engineer with the espionage, sabotage, and assassination skills of a ninja.

Nonetheless, startups everywhere advertise their need to hire a "rock-star coder" or "front-end ninja," further perpetuating the damaging myth that only a select few people are qualified to help create great products.

Identifying Top Performers Is Difficult

Interviews are a tall order. In a few hours, you're attempting to make a decision about a person with whom you hope to have a relationship for many years. You often spend as much time (or more) with your work colleagues than you do with a spouse or partner, but the courtship process is much, much shorter.

Let's assume that 10x programmers do exist. How might you successfully and repeatedly identify them in a brief interview process? Great question. Even the best, brightest, and most resource-rich minds have trouble with this one.

Laszlo Bock, the head of all people operations at Google, made waves a couple of years ago when he admitted the poor predictive quality of their interviews:

> *Years ago, we did a study to determine whether anyone at Google is particularly good at hiring. We looked at tens of thousands of interviews, and everyone who had done the interviews, and what they scored the candidate, and how that person ultimately performed in their job. We found zero relationship. It's a complete random mess, except for one guy who was highly predictive because he only interviewed people for a very specialized area, where he happened to be the world's leading expert.[3]*

Furthermore, interview techniques that have long been used in the technology industry might be misguided as well. Bock continues:

> *On the hiring side, we found that brainteasers are a complete waste of time. How many golf balls can you fit into an airplane? How many gas stations in Manhattan? A complete waste of time. They don't predict anything. They serve primarily to make the interviewer feel smart.*

Before you give up altogether and simply hire the next engineer who walks through your door, take heart that you're not the only one facing this challenge. Thinking continues to evolve, especially around the use of behavioral interviews and tests of emotional intelligence as good predictors of success. New approaches and techniques are being tried all the time, and there are ways to help identify the potential top performers for your future team—but they're definitely not perfect.

Hiring Is Hard

Finding candidates is only the first step in a long process. Next, you have to hire them.

Hiring is made complicated by several factors:

- Hiring decisions by your team are often not unanimous, especially at first. Ideally, everyone would share the same enthusiasm for a candidate, covering all the aspects of what was tested. In reality, however, it's typically much more difficult to build consensus and make decisions confidently.

---

[3]www.nytimes.com/2013/06/20/business/in-head-hunting-big-data-may-not-be-such-a-big-deal.html

- Just as you're looking for consensus on hiring decisions, the same is true of your overall hiring strategy, and people may have a wide variety of opinions. It's important to agree on a strategy before conducting interviews; otherwise, your discussions may go in circles.

- Each candidate is different. It's your responsibility to understand them as well as possible, so that you can craft the most convincing argument for why they should join your company, but this can be tricky. They may choose to withhold information, change their minds, or simply be skilled negotiators. People are complicated—there's no one approach that's guaranteed to work in all cases.

- You need to be effective in selling people on the merits of your opportunity. Great candidates have many options, and it's up to you to present your company and team in the most attractive way possible, for each specific candidate.

- Your job doesn't end when an offer is sent. You need to maintain contact and build a connection with candidates, which can be time-consuming but valuable. Help them develop an increasingly clear picture of what life will be like on your team.

Once an offer is accepted, you can finally relax, right? You've done it—landed a big fish—and now it's time to celebrate.

Not so fast.

Many things can still happen between the time an offer is accepted and the first day of work. The candidate may have a change of heart, external circumstances may force the candidate to change plans, there may be problems getting a visa or work permit, and so on. The most important thing to do is stay in close contact with the candidate throughout the entire process. This communication will also start to build your working relationship, which is valuable for your long-term success together.

Management: The Overlooked Opportunity

Creating long-term success for your organization isn't only about building a team. Fixing your recruiting and hiring process without also improving how you manage and retain engineers would be like trying to sustain a bonfire with nothing but kindling. You want your company's fire to burn hot, but also for a long time.

Engineering management, especially at startups, is far too often neglected and overlooked as a core discipline, which is good news for you. Why? Because you can outperform the market. By investing a bit of time, attention, and resources into improving the management skills and process of you and your team, you can reap long-term gains over your competitors in terms of productivity and team morale.

Compared to engineering recruiting, which is fiercely competitive, exhausting, and uncertain, managing your people effectively provides a relatively rich opportunity to deliver value.

If you're not convinced this opportunity exists, consider the following financial calculation.

Let's say your team is looking for another senior engineer, with experience in Python and the Django web framework. If you factor in the costs of a contingent recruiter bonus, onboarding time and expenses, and other general overhead for adding a new person, you might end up spending $30,000 on the hire. Maybe more.

What if you invested the same $30,000 training somebody on your team? Think about how far that money could go toward things like workshops, classes, books, online materials, and more. In some places, you might even be able to get a master's degree. Or you could spread the money out and train your whole team.

Similarly, it tends to be cheaper, overall, to keep good people than to replace them. By providing the kind of career growth, work environment, and compensation people desire, you can reduce the number of occasions in which you need to hire somebody.

What's in This Book

This book discusses the challenges of building and managing a high-performance engineering team. These challenges are paired with ideas, techniques, and strategies for making tangible progress and reaching your team-building goals.

Part 1 opens with a discussion of the engineering recruiting process. Before detailing some successful techniques, we first attempt to debunk some common myths and conventional wisdom about recruiting that limit many people and teams. After deconstructing these counterproductive tendencies, we'll discuss specific, industry-tested approaches to finding and landing top engineering talent.

Part 2 discusses the final step of recruiting: hiring. Much more than simply creating and sending an offer to a viable candidate, hiring requires preparation, strategy, and consideration of many often overlooked factors. We'll look at the challenges of hiring in more detail, outline some specific approaches to try with your team, suggest possible modifications, and build toward long-term success.

Part 3 concludes with an in-depth look at management, starting with a deceptively simple question: Do you even want to be a manager? To help you answer the question, we'll discuss the important aspects of the job, trade-offs involved with being in management, and what you can expect in the role. We'll also cover the ways in which you can get the best performance and satisfaction from your team, achieve career growth, and generally help your company succeed by practicing effective management.

About Me: Why I Wrote This Book

After several years as a professional software engineer in a variety of Silicon Valley companies, I started to develop an interest in technical management. The primary reason was simple: I disagreed with decisions being made by my superiors (or at least thought I did) and realized the only way to do something about it was to get into those conversations. This wasn't purely driven by hubris or an inflated sense of self-importance; I honestly felt I could make things better for the engineers with whom I worked. I believed we needed an advocate and representative for the technical folks on my team, and that I was the most willing and motivated to provide that service.

My first real experience in management came at a local-events web-search company called Zvents. Later acquired by eBay, Zvents was in many ways a typical fast-paced Silicon Valley venture-funded startup. At the time I became a manager, my small team of engineers was working furiously on several initiatives as the company iterated and experimented on the product. I had a lot of ideas about how my team, and the company in general, could be doing things better—and I was certainly wrong about most of them.

Over the next several years at Zvents, robotics research lab Willow Garage, and robotic telepresence startup Suitable Technologies, I gradually figured things out. Through a series of mistakes (some of which are detailed in this book), a consistent effort to learn by reading and consulting with experienced managers and leaders, and analysis of what has worked and failed in my own experience, I developed a deep appreciation for the challenges of the position and much sharper instincts about how to succeed. Only now do I believe that I truly understand what it means to build and manage a team.

As vice president of engineering and design at Course Hero, the world's leading crowd-sourced educational materials platform, I'm able to apply this knowledge and experience on a daily basis. With the support of our chief executive officer (CEO) Andrew Grauer, we've created a team that's productive, sustainable, growing fast, and a joy to be part of.

I don't look at the information in this book as part of a zero-sum game. By sharing what I've learned, I hope to make others more effective in their work, help build value in interesting new companies, and, perhaps most important, make engineers around the world just a little bit happier.

Recruiting

An Enlightened Approach to Recruiting

The first step in constructing your engineering team is recruiting some great people to join you.

For too many people and companies, recruiting is an afterthought. It's considered an unavoidable nuisance that stands between you and having a productive team of builders who share your passion and vision for creating a great company.

Almost everyone starts by thinking this way, and I suppose it's understandable. For many people, their first experience with recruiting is as the target of a recruiter's search. If you've worked in a technical field for any length of time, you've probably been contacted many times by recruiters about positions that are clearly not of interest, and these recruiters can waste your time because they haven't done much research on who you actually are or what you actually want to do.

Unfortunately, most recruiters take a scattershot, or "spray and pray," approach, contacting as many people as possible and hoping to get a few nibbles. Being on the receiving end of these queries will understandably make you cynical about the recruiting process in general. And LinkedIn, as the most popular medium for these requests, has developed a bit of a reputation as a magnet for recruiting spam.

As we'll discuss later, this broken, frustrating system is an outgrowth of the contingent recruiting model. A contingent recruiter is paid only when a candidate is successfully hired, in the form of a bonus that's typically a percentage of the new hire's starting salary.

The appeal of contingent recruiting is obvious: You pay only for results. It aligns well with the thinking that recruiting isn't an important function of your company, only a necessary evil that must be completed in order to move on. It requires very little investment on the part of the hiring manager, who simply enjoys the results at the end.

Startup founders and hiring managers know they need developers, and they want to hire somebody to solve this problem for them, so they can stay focused on their own work of laying out the product roadmap and planning business objectives.

Or at least, that's the idea.

The downside of contingent recruiting is that it creates a poor alignment of incentives between the hiring manager, recruiter, and candidates. It rewards the shotgun approach to contacting candidates, which creates a lot of extra work for the hiring manager, who must sort through lots of poorly-matched candidates, as well as the candidates themselves, who have to deal with tons of incoming requests that are a waste of their time.

Fortunately, there are better ways to build your team—models that properly align the incentives of everyone involved, including the recruiters themselves. Furthermore, the role of the recruiter is only one small part in the overall effort required to find and hire great people.

Companies that do this well, over long periods of time, and have structured their team, process, and culture to maximize their chances of success, are the ones I believe have achieved *recruiting enlightenment.*

This chapter introduces the philosophy of enlightened recruiting. We'll briefly discuss important cultural aspects of successful recruiting, including how you should think about your role in creating a recruiting strategy, and we'll set the stage for a deeper tactical discussion in the following chapters.

What Is Recruiting Enlightenment?

An enlightened approach to recruiting includes the following:

- Recruiting is a first-order company and business priority, equivalent to (or even ahead of) building the product, booking sales, or anything else you consider highly important. Recruiting never takes a back seat.

- Your company is committed to building expertise in recruiting. Rather than looking to outsource a solution, you invest the time and resources necessary to develop deep knowledge, skill, and intuition about recruiting through your organization. You may (and probably should) engage with external parties for education and help, but never as a complete substitute. No short cuts.

- You value and reward individual contributions to the overall recruiting effort. These rewards may take the form of referral bonuses, consideration in performance reviews, recognition in public settings, or others. However you choose to do it, you should make sure that everyone considers a contribution to recruiting something to be celebrated and part of doing a great job.

- Everyone is involved in recruiting. Everyone. Each department or team in your company should have an idea of how they can help.

- Recruiting is an integral part of your company culture. It may even appear in your mission statement or goals.

- You hire people who care about recruiting and will be enthusiastic about helping you do it better. For each prospective hire, you consider their ability to attract, directly or indirectly, more great people to the company.

- You're willing to experiment with your recruiting and see what works—to take the extra time and resources to try different things, analyze the results, and never settle with the status quo.

Enlightenment does not come easily, but can be incredibly valuable. The effort invested in learning the skills necessary for successful recruiting will pay off in meaningful, profound ways over the life of your company and your career hiring engineers.

Get Your Hands Dirty

Most hiring managers would prefer not to invest the time required to understand and perfect the recruiting process, and they would certainly prefer not to do it themselves. Getting your hands dirty, however, is a critical part of achieving recruiting enlightenment.

Chapter 4 covers a number of techniques and ideas to help improve your recruiting success. An important prerequisite for these, or any other recruiting approaches, to work is for you (the hiring manager) to first implement them yourself. Don't tell someone else what to try—do it yourself, refine the idea, and then, only when you're sure that it's working, instruct others on how to proceed.

To put it in engineering terms: Prototype the solution, iterate rapidly, and when you're satisfied with the results, look to scale it up quickly.

When I started as VP of Engineering at Course Hero, I was given a clear mandate to scale up the technical team as fast as possible. Based on my previous years of experience, I was confident we could do it, but I was also aware that the current team had struggled quite a bit with the task. (This was, of course, why I was hired.)

The engineers at Course Hero had contracted with several contingency-based recruiters to bring them candidates. As I described, this appears to be a logical strategy.

What transpired, however, was also what I described—the team was stuck in a quagmire of mediocre candidates, wasting tons of engineer time and building a growing sense of frustration and cynicism with the process.

After taking stock of the situation, my first step was basically to push the reset button. We cancelled every existing contingent recruiter agreement (with one exception), gave up our non-technical in-house candidate screener, and took over the entire process. For the next month, I spent all of my available time searching for candidates directly, doing all phone screens and initial interviews, and coordinating the entire interview process.

If this sounds like a lot of work, it was. But after a month or so, I had a much better idea of the answers to the following critical questions:

- What sources are the most productive in terms of finding qualified candidates?

- Within these sources, what search terms and filters produce the best matches?

- What candidate attributes correlate most strongly with success in our interviews and work performance, when hired?

- Is our interview process effective in filtering out poor candidates and selecting good ones?

- Are we asking the right questions in our interviews?

After a month or two, we were starting to see some improvements. The overall number of interviews had gone down, and the quality had gone up, making recruiting much less burdensome and frustrating for the team. And, of course, we had started hiring some good new people.

At this point, it was time to start scaling things up. This meant primarily two things:

- Bringing more engineers into the process, so that they could help evaluate candidates and conduct interviews. I couldn't do the whole thing forever.

- Finding some recruiters, either internally or externally, who could understand, replicate, and even improve the process I had established, broadening our reach and increasing our candidate flow without compromising the quality.

Chapter 4 covers much more detail on how to find and work with effective recruiters, but you can probably guess by now that I don't recommend the contingency-based model. Once you're enlightened about recruiting, you'll appreciate that the way to hire a recruiter is similar to hiring nearly any other professional—you do the research to find somebody who is skilled at the craft and pay them for their time. Yes, you'll spend a lot of money before making any hires, but in the long term, with properly aligned incentives, you should see much better results. (If you don't, you chose the wrong recruiter.)

Furthermore, with your own personal experience, you'll be more effective in guiding recruiters toward what works, building a truly collaborative relationship.

Recruiting as a Core Company Principle

Course Hero's engineering team has five core principles that guide our activities and influence individual decision-making:

- Ship Early and Often
- Only One Project at a Time
- Testing Is a First-Class Activity
- Communicate Openly and Frequently
- Always Be Recruiting

As you can see, recruiting is up there with everything else. It's just as important to our culture, both now and in the future, as anything related to development or technical work.

By "Always Be Recruiting," we mean that engineers, along with everyone else in the company, should be looking for every opportunity to find, entice, and land great people for our teams. Every interaction with someone outside the company is an opportunity to spread positive information into the world, or to connect, even if it's the beginning of a second- or third-degree link, with somebody who might be interested and able to help you out.

If you think about recruiting only during predefined, isolated times, you're missing out on countless serendipitous opportunities to make valuable connections. Most of them won't go anywhere. But some of them will—even if they take months or years—and you won't know ahead of time which those will be. Keep your mind in recruiting mode at all times, and train your team to do the same.

Summary

Don't let bad previous experience make you cynical about the prospects of recruiting great engineers to your team. In the next two chapters, we'll cover in detail how to create a winning strategy, common pitfalls to avoid, and specific techniques that will help your team unlock its next level of growth.

CHAPTER 3

Six Destructive Myths About Technical Recruiting

Before we discuss the details of how to build a recruiting strategy, we need to dismantle the destructive thinking that surrounds technical recruiting today. This chapter details six specific misconceptions about recruiting and proposes some alternate ways of thinking.

Myth 1: You Need to Find More Candidates

Almost everyone has the same idea about how to solve the hiring problem: find more candidates. It's easy to see why—filling the top of the funnel is a simple way to increase your hiring output without changing anything about your philosophy and process. It also allows you to outsource the work required, typically to third-party recruiters.

Here's my response:

Finding more candidates is the hardest possible way to solve your hiring problem.

Of course this approach can work, but you should look for some easier and more cost-effective alternatives as well. The first step is to identify things you're doing to artificially limit the pool of possible candidates. Myths 2–5 contain more detail on this topic and common hiring pitfalls.

Second, you may not be considering all the ways to take advantage of your current resources. Instead of focusing everything on hiring a senior iOS engineer, is there someone on your team who could get there in a few months with the right amount of support and training? It may end up being cheaper and faster, when you consider the time taken and recruiter bonuses paid out, to train someone into the role than hire externally.

Finally, you may not need *more* candidates; you may need *better* candidates. Your recruiting process, and the people helping you with it, may not be the right ones for the challenge.

We want to make recruiting and hiring as deterministic as we can. Read on.

Myth 2: Dealing with Visas Is Too Hard

Earlier in my career, I viewed employment visas as an intractable problem. In my first experience as a manager, I assumed that hiring people from other countries was going to be expensive, difficult, and risky. Every situation is different, but none of these things is necessarily true. The trick is learning to recognize and handle all the situations that come up.

Learning how to recruit, hire, and manage people who require sponsorship to work in the United States is different from what you might be used to, however. They have different concerns, requirements, and considerations, some of which might be surprising or even counterintuitive to you. The ability to maintain their visa status, or work toward a green card and citizenship, will often trump just about everything else, including compensation or job details. Furthermore, requirements are placed on them by their visas that you might not fully understand. For example, an H-1B (one of the most common work visas) makes it difficult for a spouse to find work, which puts additional pressure on an employee with a family to be a stable provider.

Yes, navigating the visa process is a lot of work and costs money, but if you're trying to recruit and hire without investing any money or effort, you need to reset your expectations immediately. When it comes to finding great people for your team, this is an investment worth making, and the first step is to find an immigration attorney who can help you.

Chapter 4 goes into a lot more detail about the various types of visas, considerations when recruiting and hiring people who require a visa, and specific recommendations for your own strategy.

Myth 3: Algorithmic Knowledge Trumps Everything

One day, my team was deep in an unusually long hiring meeting about a particular candidate. We were stuck in a bit of a hiring drought, and it seemed like a lot of people we interviewed just weren't quite good enough.

Not wanting cynicism to overtake the process, I polled the team about the qualities most important to them in a prospective candidate. The list was as long as it was interesting, and I was surprised by the wide range of attributes people care about. The top five are listed in the following sidebar.

FIVE ATTRIBUTES TO LOOK FOR IN SOFTWARE CANDIDATES

1. The candidate has something to teach me, such as new skills, techniques, or conventions. I will learn and grow in my own work by virtue of this person being on my team.

2. The candidate loves programming and technology. They share my enthusiasm for creating great software and building a product.

3. The candidate is pleasant to be around. They take feedback well, collaborate with others, know when to ask for help, are open to learning new things and ways to work, and have multiple interests.

4. The candidate takes pride in their work. They have an attention to detail, aim to make a great product, and emphasize code readability and reuse.

5. The candidate thinks entrepreneurially. They think about how to improve all aspects of a product and company, and are proactive about problem solving.

Notice anything missing that you might have expected? How about, "The candidate can implement merge sort"? Conspicuously absent is any kind of technical test or algorithmic puzzle.

Clearly, we require a minimum set of technical skills in order to trust someone to add to our code base safely and without creating mountains of future problems. But perhaps we're overweighting the importance of those skills in the grand scheme of things? Silicon Valley giants like Google and Facebook are famously algorithm-heavy in their interviews, choosing to do most of their interaction at a whiteboard (we'll come back to this topic later), and many smaller companies have made the totally rational decision to emulate their technique. But what's right for them may not be right for you. If you're a small startup, you have different factors to consider.

In particular, a large company needs to make sure its interview results are consistent—across time, location, interview team, and a lot of other variables—and in some ways are reduced to the lowest common denominator in their process. Algorithmic knowledge is more empirical than almost anything else you can test. If your team is small, you have the opportunity to create a more insightful interview process. Take advantage of it.

Furthermore, influential works such as *The Mythical Man-Month* have entrenched the idea of a 10x programmer—a software engineer who is (at least) 10 times more productive than an "average" engineer.[1] This ongoing debate is spirited on both sides, but no matter which side is right, this topic has affected how teams conduct interviews. If you're looking to find someone 10 times better than average, what kind of questions can you ask? How you determine if their communication skills are 10x? Or their personality?

Teams have gravitated toward algorithmic questions because they lend themselves more readily to a mathematical, empirical comparison of candidates. By measuring runtime complexity, time to complete a task, lines of code written, or bug rate, for example, you can decide whether someone is 10 times better in this dimension. The danger is in extrapolating this thinking to also decide that they're 10 times better as an engineer, overall.

Which is related to…

Myth 4: You Need to Find People with Experience

Some experience is required, yes, but probably not as much as you think.

I don't intend to debate the particular requirements of the jobs you're trying to fill, since every situation is different. My point, which applies to almost every one of these situations, though, is this:

If you find yourself rejecting candidates primarily because they need more experience, consider making an investment in providing that experience yourself.

---

[1] Frederick Brooks, *The Mythical Man-Month: Essays on Software Engineering*, 2nd Edition. Addison-Wesley Professional, 1995: p. 30.

Sure, it would be great for people to be fully productive from day one. More realistically, however, figure out how to invest more in training. For example:

- Develop a training or onboarding program for new hires.
- Encourage or require pair programming for more knowledge transfer.
- Add some slack into the product timeline, allowing for more learning.

These, and related ideas, are discussed in more detail in Chapter 4.

Were you fully qualified for every new role you started? Did someone ever take a chance on you? Calculated risks are intrinsic to all parts of the startup experience, and hiring is no exception.

Furthermore, if you take the same amount of time, money, and effort required to find a great, experienced employee, and put that into training and mentorship for people you already have, you might be able to *create* an experienced employee rather than find one.

Myth 5: You Need to Find Local People

The San Francisco Bay Area houses approximately 7 million people. By my math, that's approximately 0.1 percent of the world population. Even if you account for the relative concentration of skilled technical and creative people, it's still a small slice of the world's talent. By comparison, how well would your business run if you threw away 99.9 percent of your sales leads?

Once you've decided to expand your search geography, you'll have to decide an important cultural question:

How important is it for your people to work in the same physical location?

Consider it carefully, as it's one of the most important decisions you'll ever make. Both options have pros and cons (and elicit strong opinions). Let's consider each side of the argument.

Why You Should Build a Local Team

In 2013, Yahoo CEO Marissa Mayer made waves by ending Yahoo's liberal work-from-home policy. Many employees valued the flexibility the policy offered, but for a company struggling to find a new, more relevant identity, Mayer felt it was an important step. From the Yahoo internal memo:

> *To become the absolute best place to work, communication and collaboration will be important, so we need to be working side-by-side. That is why it is critical that we are all present in our offices. Some of the best decisions and insights come from hallway and cafeteria discussions, meeting new people, and impromptu team meetings. Speed and quality are often sacrificed when we work from home. We need to be one Yahoo!, and that starts with physically being together.[2]*

Many other companies have succeeded while placing the same importance on being together. Google now has over 50,000 employees spread over 70 offices worldwide, but still demonstrates a strong preference for bringing its top technical talent to Mountain View. Individual productivity may be higher when working remotely, but if communication and collaboration are paramount for your team's work culture, you can't do any better than having everyone in the same physical space.

Why You Should Build a Distributed Team

The controversy over Mayer's remarks show just how divisive this issue can be. Many companies have also built large, successful teams in an entirely distributed fashion.

The primary advantage is obvious: you have a much larger pool of people from which to recruit. Not everyone wants to live near your office, or is willing and able to relocate, even for a great opportunity.

There are secondary advantages as well: by creating a culture that supports remote and distributed work, many people feel grateful for the unique opportunity it provides them to work for your company in a way that affords them more flexibility in their personal lives. This freedom can be abused as well, but when done right, creates a positive environment. The key to this approach is to get the right tools and processes in place, and make sure they're consistently and appropriately used.

---

[2]Nicholas Carlson, *Marissa Mayer and the Fight to Save Yahoo!* Twelve, 2015: p. 262.

It's critical that every team member, no matter where they sit, has the same information, access, and influence they would have anywhere else. Chat apps such as Slack and HipChat are invaluable, as are other electronic tools for communication, project management, and supporting technical development. Videoconferencing, in particular, is useful in creating shared understanding and context, as is the next iteration of that particular technology: the telepresence robot.[3]

Myth 6: You Should Avoid Recruiters

Like any field, technical recruiting is full of a variety of people. They're not all the same.

If you're working with a bad recruiter—one who is wasting your time or doesn't have your best interests at heart—you haven't put enough effort into finding a good one.

Working in technical recruiting is a lot like real estate. There are low barriers to entry, the potential upside is high (and typically commission based), and communication and networking skills are essential. As in real estate, this attracts a wide variety of people to the field, and you need to quickly separate the ones who can help you from the ones who can't.

How to find and work with great recruiters is covered in the next chapter. Don't be scared off by the price tag or stories you may have heard from others. Recruiters are an indispensable resource for building your team in a competitive environment.

Summary

Recruiting software engineers to your team is difficult, arduous work. By breaking down some of the common myths that limit success in this endeavor, you can maximize the return on your investment of time and money into recruiting.

---

[3]For further reading on the nascent telepresence robotics industry, I recommend Parmy Olson's overview, "Rise Of The Telepresence Robots," in the July 15, 2013 issue of *Forbes* magazine.

Nine Steps to Recruiting Success

Developing a winning recruiting strategy takes time and effort. It can seem overwhelming, so let's break it down into specific steps. Here's what we'll cover:

- Prepare Yourself for the Grind
- Prepare to Spend
- Identify the Top Qualities to Look For
- Make Your Company Attractive
- Learn Where to Look for Engineers
- Develop a Strategy for Visas
- Develop Your Training Program
- Find a Recruiter
- Establish Long-Term Solutions

The steps are discussed in roughly the order you'll want to address them, although obviously every situation is different. Let's get started.

Step #1: Prepare Yourself for The Grind

Recruiting isn't magic. It's not really even an art. It's a grind. A full-court press. It requires the willingness to do anything and everything, all the time, to maximize your chances of success. The first step on your path to recruiting success is to reset your expectations and prepare yourself for "The Grind".

For arduous or repetitive tasks, this means coming up with a work style or pattern that you can sustain. If you're the one searching LinkedIn and contacting candidates, set aside a portion of every day for this task. Don't let yourself procrastinate the task away, or let it be trumped by seemingly more urgent things that will inevitably come up. Set goals based on quantity for this time, such as the examples shown in the sidebar.

EXAMPLES OF QUANTITATIVE RECRUITING GOALS

- Contact at least five new candidates
- Spend 30 minutes searching LinkedIn or other job boards
- Spend 10 minutes with each person on your team, asking them about potential contacts
- Post jobs on at least three different boards

Creative professionals know the importance of quantitative goals and how they can lead to qualitative results. A writer might write several thousand words a week, every week, even without a compelling topic. A photographer might try for 250 photos per day. Regular practice leads to mastery, but even more important, it increases the chances of having one spectacular success. The more chips you can spread around the roulette table, the higher the likelihood you'll hit a winner.

So, like the artist toiling away at his craft without a clear result in mind, you need to be persistent, disciplined, and trust that in time, success will be yours.

Similarly, you need to prioritize your recruiting activities above everything else you do. Yes, everything. Speed is essential. Candidates will pick up on your responsiveness, as it's an indicator of how truly interested you are, and how much you care about their interests and goals.

Big companies take a long time to usher candidates through their lengthy hiring processes. Use this lethargy to create a competitive advantage for yourself. People want to go where they feel appreciated, and one of the best ways you can do that is to stay engaged and, indeed, aggressive throughout the entire process.

Whenever an action or information is required from you, make sure you handle it within 24 hours. Aim to go from initial contact to a hiring decision within seven days. If a candidate can come in tomorrow (when you're busy) or next Tuesday (which is open for you), find a way to make it happen tomorrow.

Welcome to The Grind.

Step #2: Prepare to Spend

If you want to build a top-notch engineering team in today's competitive tech market, you're going to have to spend some money. There are different ways to spend it, but almost everything you can do to increase your chances of success is going to come with a price tag. There's no free lunch here—the less expensive approaches require more time and effort.

How much will it cost? That depends on how urgent and specific your hiring needs are. The upper bound would be a 25 percent contingent recruiter bonus, but as you'll see later, I think there are better options. My rule of thumb is that, for each hire, expect to invest at least $10,000, 100 hours of your time, or some combination of the two. To put it in a formula:

$$X \text{ of your dollars} + Y*100 \text{ of your hours} >= 10,000$$

Where does the money go? Lots of places, if you look at the entire task of finding, hiring, and getting a new person started on your team.

Table 4-1 shows some approximate numbers for how much various aspects of recruiting and hiring cost, per hire.

Table 4-1. Approximate Recruiting and Hiring Costs

Recruiting Expense	Approximate Cost
Contingent recruiter fees	20-40K
Contract recruiter fees	5K-15K
In-house recruiter compensation	5K-10K
Interview trips	1K-2K
Visa applications	2K-10K
Relocation	2K-10K
Referral bonuses	1K-5K
Job board postings	500-1K
Web site improvements	1K-2K

Even if you don't incur all of these costs for each hire, you can see that it adds up quickly.

One encouraging thing to keep in mind is that your first few hires are likely to be your most expensive. When you start a search to fill a new position, there are ramp-up costs—in both time and money—but as you develop effective recruiting channels and screening filters, the average cost per hire will decrease. If you're working with a recruiter, they'll build a stronger sense of what you're looking for as well, thereby decreasing the time (and cost) to make a hire.

Step #3: Identify the Top Qualities to Look For

Conventional wisdom in Silicon Valley is that you need to find ninja-rockstar-superstar engineers, mythical creatures that are only occasionally seen in real life. Some even use the term "unicorn" to emphasize this status. Hiring anything less will consign your company to eternal mediocrity. This thinking has led to Chapter 3's third myth, Algorithmic Knowledge Trumps Everything.

While this knowledge may in fact be the most important thing for your team (for example, if you're building a team of quantitative analysts for a high-frequency trading hedge fund), don't start by assuming it to be true. Take a long look at what qualities are the most valuable to you, discuss it with your team, and build consensus about what the ideal candidate actually looks like.

A good way to start is to look at recent successful hires and see what qualities stand out in those people. What aspects of their personality or skillset make them successful? How can you find or evaluate those qualities in new candidates? Make a list and use it to help craft your interview plans. In hiring discussions, refer back to the list, asking for your team's opinions on how it applies to the candidate.

In Chapter 3, we debunked the supremacy of algorithmic knowledge as a hiring signal and discussed some other characteristics to consider instead. These, and others your team comes up with, may be very useful in identifying great candidates whom you might otherwise have overlooked.

Teachability

In my years of hiring, however, one particular quality stands out above all others in predicting the success of a prospective software engineering candidate: *Teachability*.

Similarly, it's the factor that also rules out more candidates than any other.

Every new hire is going to spend time learning and growing into a new position. No one is a perfect fit right away. The question, therefore, is, how much of an investment do you need to make in this person, and how much will it pay off? Junior candidates will likely require more mentorship than senior ones, but in both cases, some will be required. Even experienced candidates will need to do some amount of learning—about how your team does things, where their experience can best help, and the nuances of your product and business. Skilled programmers will need to learn your engineering process, codebase, and conventions.

At all levels, the interest and aptitude for learning are a strong, clear signal for how well someone will do in your organization.

Your company is growing, and you want people who will grow with you. Think beyond the challenges of today. You need people who will learn in ways that enable them to solve the problems of tomorrow.

Finally, in all my companies, and especially at Course Hero, we've found that we just generally like being around people who love to learn. It's a wonderful, infectious spirit that's ideally suited for teams that are on the rise. Culturally, it's a good fit for the kind of environment you want to foster.

So how do you determine if someone is teachable?

Throughout your interview process, look for signs that your mentorship of the candidate will be productive. Let's break it down into two separate but important questions:

- Is this person capable of learning?
- Is this person interested in learning?

You need to be confident that the answer to both questions is "yes." Here are some specific things to look for:

- Does the candidate receive and incorporate feedback from the interviewer? If you suggest a way to approach a problem, do they listen? You should be clear that you're not trying to trap them with trick questions. See how they respond to your feedback and incorporate it into their work.

- Does the candidate apply things discussed earlier in the interview to subsequent questions or problems? This is a great way for them to demonstrate that they've learned something and are receptive to feedback.

- Does the candidate communicate well and have an active dialogue as you work through problems? Effective communication during the interview suggests that you can look forward to productive work sessions with this person.

- Is the candidate able to talk about past projects where they've tried to learn things beyond strictly what was asked of them? Have they shown that they're self-motivated to learn, improve, and share knowledge with others?

Being "teachable" means that a person is receptive to testing out and trying new approaches. The people on your team will be mentors and colleagues for any new hires, and will want to share their knowledge and perspectives. The willingness to learn, and to consider new approaches to solving problems, will be highly valued by your team, and will help them embrace a potential new teammate.

Whether you decide that teachability is your top, must-have quality, or something else is, the most important thing you must to do is develop a clear picture of what you're actually looking for in a candidate, and how it correlates with on-the-job success.

Step #4: Make Your Company Attractive

First impressions make a big difference. Imagine you're selling a house. Would you spend thousands of dollars on marketing, trying to drum up interest for an open house to show it off, and then neglect to mow the lawn or make sure the windows are clean? Of course not. To borrow a phrase from the real estate industry, you want to make sure your company has *curb appeal*.

Your Web Site

The first place to consider is your company web site, as it's typically the first place an applicant will go to learn more about an opportunity, whether they were referred by a friend or found you on a job board. Does your site convey the correct impression of what it's like to work there, and provide a positive signal to the kind of person you want to hire?

Candidates now often look for information about company culture before the details of a particular role. More than knowing what they will do at your company, they want to know why they will love doing it. Job descriptions for software engineering positions all start to look the same after you've seen a few, and most candidates already have a pretty good idea of the day-to-day details—writing code, shipping product, fine-tuning your application stack, and so on. To pique the interest of a potential applicant, therefore, you need to focus on the peripherals. For example:

- How does your team communicate? What tools do you use?

- How do you foster collaboration?

- What new things will new employees learn if they work there?

- How do people grow in their careers? Are there examples?

- Why is working there fun?

Similarly, don't go overboard highlighting all your fancy perks, unless they truly are unique. These don't set you apart and just take up space and attention that could be used to express what does make you unique. As Ben Horowitz writes, "Every smart company values their employees. Perks are good, but they are not culture."[1] In crafting your online presence for potential employees, focus on your *culture*.

Humans respond positively to other humans. Showcase your team and give it a human feel. Nobody dreams of working for a faceless, unfeeling corporate monolith. Even if your company is huge, there are smiling, caring people making it tick. Show that to the world.

The "About Us" page is critical, and under no circumstances should you consider skipping or shortchanging it. People have learned that this is the first stop to learn more about the actual people in company. And on this page, the first person they will read about is the CEO. Culture flows downhill, so it's essential that you project a CEO persona that fits with your core values and will inspire confidence about what your company is truly like.

Some companies show personal profiles only for senior management, and some aim to have equal billing for every single employee. Both approaches are fine, but keep in mind that it's important to keep the page up to date. Having incorrect or outdated information on your site chips away at your credibility.

This may seem self-evident, but it's also essential to have an accurate, current list of your job openings on your site. You don't want to turn away talented people simply because you haven't gotten around to adding that new mobile developer position yet. Some people will contact you to see if there's an opportunity for something that isn't explicitly listed—but most people won't.

Your job descriptions should also lead off with information about company culture, selling people on why you're such a uniquely fun and exciting place to work. The job requirements come at the end. Why? For many applicants, this

---

[1]www.bhorowitz.com/programming_your_culture

may be the first thing they see. For example, they might receive a direct link to a particular job listing from a friend, or click through to a listing from a job site. Maybe they'll eventually click over to your "About Us" page or other company pages, but maybe they won't.

Always be selling. Use every opportunity to convince people that you have a great place to work. Even if it doesn't work out for them, they may pass this information on to somebody else.

Most job descriptions focus too much on simply what the company wants. "Five years Java experience." "CS degree." "Proven track record of shipping great products." What most are missing is a description of what somebody will accomplish by working there. For example, instead of this:

> *Candidate must have two years of experience building web applications with Django.*

Try something like this:

> *As part of our team, you'll leverage your experience in building Django web apps to help architect the next generation of features in our 2.0 product.*

Always be selling. Make it sound interesting. Assume you want to get everybody who reads your description to be excited about the opportunity.

Profiles on Other Sites

Once you've added slick, enticing job descriptions to your own web site, replicate them on other sites where people might be looking for jobs. In particular, use AngelList and LinkedIn.

Make sure that your company profiles, and all job descriptions on other sites, are accurate and kept up-to-date. Check that you've included all the appropriate keywords that a good candidate might be using to search. Assume that the first thing somebody will do, after seeing a job post from your company, is click through to your profile on that site. Don't lose them at that step.

Step #5: Learn Where to Look for Engineers

When you start your search, your ideal candidate will be:

- Local to your office
- From a top 10 school
- Looking for a job

- Passionate about your product or market
- Highly experienced in the skills you need

Unfortunately, unless you're Google or Facebook, you've narrowed the population down to essentially zero. To have success, you're going to have to compromise on at least one of these criteria.

I suggest you expand your search in two ways:

- Look outside your local area
- Look for students or alumni from the "second tier" of engineering schools

Recruiting Remotely

First, you need to decide that you're willing to recruit from other regions. This means, by extension, that you're willing to either pay for people to relocate to you or build a distributed team. Both can work—but you should be clear on what your strategy is.

If you're trying to build a local, co-located team, then obviously you'll need to relocate people.

- Be clear about your expectations. Make sure people know that they will be expected to relocate, if offered a job. Don't let that be a surprise at the end.

- Be clear about what you cover. State your relocation policy up front, so candidates aren't worried about the potential costs.

- Be generous. Paying to relocate somebody is almost always going to be much less than a recruiter fee, and well within the range of what you should be expecting to pay for a hire.

There are some tools that can help you identify people who not only are willing to relocate, but might actually be excited to do it. Obviously, being in a highly-desirable location, such as San Francisco, makes this more likely.

AngelList (http://angel.co) is a great resource for finding people interested in startups, and it has some useful and powerful search tools for both candidates and employers. In particular, it offers a search filter called "Will Move To," shown in Figure 4-1, that lets you select individuals who have explicitly expressed a desire to move to your location.

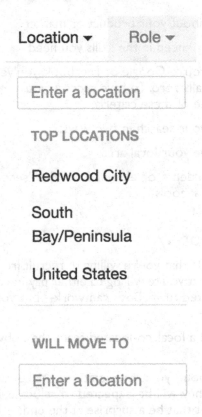

Figure 4-1. AngelList "Will Move To" input

LinkedIn, the most popular tool for finding candidates, doesn't have quite so precise a filter. Even so, you can be creative. For example, search for profiles with the term "relocate". More than a few people will have indicated their willingness to move in their profile description.

The next level of searching is to target your efforts at other, remote locations. Keep in mind that as you do so, your chances of success go down, and the effort required goes up. You're targeting a minority of the population, so you have to go through a lot more people to find the right ones. This is a good time to remember that you're in The Grind.

Rather than recruiting from *everywhere*, pick one or two specific areas to focus on. Research local companies, communities, and other resources that you would know about if you were located there. For example, if you're in San Francisco, you might target your searches at, let's say, Salt Lake City. The University of Utah has a great Computer Science department, there are a number of successful technology companies in the region, and there are thriving open source software and developer communities. If you're just a little bit lucky, you'll find a few folks who are curious about what it would be like to live and work in Silicon Valley or San Francisco, or who are willing to work remotely in a distributed team.

Searching other locations is also a good way to leverage the effort of a contract or in-house recruiter. Point them at a few places to target and see what happens. They'll have more time than you to cast a wide net and see what's caught.

When recruiting in other locations, remember to be up front about your expectations, in terms of relocation or remote work. It's not fair to a candidate to spring this information on them midway through the process.

When hiring remote employees into a distributed team, there are some good resources available. Sites such as We Work Remotely (https://weworkre-motely.com/) and the Hacker News (https://news.ycombinator.com/) "Who's Hiring?" threads have an emphasis on remote work, and good communities of people looking for these opportunities. Searching AngelList and LinkedIn can also be targeted at people looking for remote work. Figure 4-2 shows the AngelList search filter to find such people.

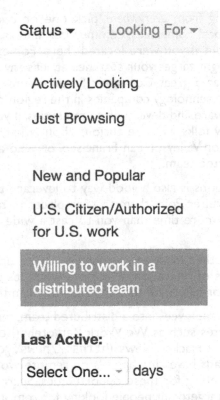

Figure 4-2. AngelList "Willing to Work in a Distributed Team" search filter

For companies in the United States, searching for people in other countries can also be productive, but make sure you understand all the visa, immigration, and other considerations before you get started.

The "Second Tier"

Recruiting engineering students directly from school, or in their first one or two years of work, is a great way to find highly talented people with a lot of growth potential. When recruiting new college graduates to your company, it's tempting to go after the top schools. This makes a lot of sense. You want the best and brightest to come in and help lead your company into the future.

There may actually be more opportunity, however, in the next layer—say, anywhere from 11 to 50, and beyond. While all the big companies and deep-pocketed recruiters go after MIT and Stanford, there are lots of really talented, bright people at places like Georgia Tech, Michigan, and the UC schools.

For example, here are the top 10 U.S. Computer Science schools in the most recent *US News & World Report* rankings:

- Carnegie Mellon University

- Massachusetts Institute of Technology

- Stanford University

- University of California—Berkeley

- University of Illinois—Urbana-Champaign

- Cornell University

- University of Washington

- Princeton University

- Georgia Institute of Technology

- University of Texas—Austin

Visit a job fair at any of those schools and I bet you'll see a huge recruiting contingent from Google, Facebook, and other name-brand tech companies. It can be hard to stand out in a crowd like that. But let's look at the next 38, schools ranked 11-48:

California Institute of Technology	University of Wisconsin—Madison
University of California—Los Angeles	University of Michigan—Ann Arbor
Columbia University	University of California—San Diego
University of Maryland—College Park	Harvard University
University of Pennsylvania	Brown University
Purdue University—West Lafayette	Rice University
University of Southern California	Yale University
Duke University	Univ. of North Carolina—Chapel Hill
Johns Hopkins University	New York University
Pennsylvania State University—University Park	University of California—Irvine
University of Minnesota—Twin Cities	University of Virginia
Northwestern University	Ohio State University
Rutgers, The State University of New Jersey—New Brunswick	University of California—Davis
University of California—Santa Barbara	University of Chicago

(*continued*)

Dartmouth College	Stony Brook University—SUNY
Texas A&M University—College Station	University of Arizona
University of Colorado—Boulder	University of Utah
Virginia Tech	Washington University in St. Louis
Arizona State University	Boston University
North Carolina State University	

Each of those schools has a lot of great candidates too. They might not be as plentiful, but they're there. And a school like Ohio State is so much larger than, say, Stanford, that in absolute terms you may actually find *more* people there. If your screening and hiring process is sound, and you're willing to put in a little effort, you'll have a lot of success expanding your horizons and your pool of candidates.

Step #6: Develop a Strategy for Visas

It's no secret that some of the best and brightest engineers are from outside the United States. If you really want to put together the best team possible, at some point you're going to have to hire someone who requires a work visa. The registration and legal fees can add up, but still usually end up being less than our upper-bound recruiter bonus. Perhaps even more daunting are the myriad options and complex rules that govern the process. There are many types of visas, each with their own criteria and restrictions.

For all of these reasons and more, your first step in creating a visa strategy should be to *find an immigration attorney*—someone who can help you and your prospective employees through the process, minimize your administrative burden, and maximize your chances of success. (This is probably the right time to point out that *this book's author is not a lawyer*.)

You should plan to offer the services of your attorney to the people you hire. Both you and your employees have the same goal in mind, and you're best off having an attorney who knows all of the relevant information on both sides. Consider it part of your recruiting expenses.

There are many types of visas, but here are the ones you're most likely to encounter or find useful in building a startup:

- H1-B
- TN (for Canadians and Mexicans)
- E-3 (for Australians)

- F-1 / OPT-STEM
- J-1
- Green Card (Permanent Residence)

Here's a quick overview of each. Please keep in mind that the laws and regulations surrounding U.S. immigration policy can change frequently, so it's always wise to check for the latest information.

H-1B

Probably the most commonly discussed of all U.S. work visas, the H-1B is a three-year visa for foreign workers in specialized fields, which generally includes engineering or development jobs. Availability for this visa is strictly limited, and often exhausted before the end of each year.

Key facts about the H-1B:

- There's a yearly limit of 65,000 granted visas, plus an additional 20,000 for applicants holding Masters degrees. (There are also some other uncommon exceptions.)

- If there are more than 65,000 applicants in the initial filing period, a lottery is held to determine whose applications are accepted. In 2014, for example, 172,500 applications were received by April.

- Once the limit has been hit, that's it for the year. Consider the following example: You have a candidate who will need a new H-1B visa. It's June, and you discover that the annual cap has already been reached. You simply won't be able to hire that person (on an H-1B) until at least the following year, when you can apply for that year's lottery.

- To be included in the lottery, the H-1B petition must be filed during the first week in April. Even if the petition is selected in the lottery and approved, the H-1B employment cannot begin until the following October 1. (Normally, this wait is not a problem for recent grads, who may have authorization to work for any employer in their field for at least 12, and up to 29, months.)

- An H-1B can generally only be extended once, for a total of six years. However, this six-year limit can be extended by starting the Green Card process (specifically, getting an approved I-140 Immigrant Petition), until a decision is made on the Green Card application. This is one reason why Green Card sponsorship is so valuable to provide. Not only does it provide a path to permanent residence, it also extends the life of the H-1B.

- A person who is already in H-1B status (e.g., working for another employer) is not subject to the annual cap, and can be hired immediately (as soon as the H-1B petition can be prepared and filed).

- If an employee is terminated while on an H-1B, they may have to leave the country. There is no guaranteed "grace period." However, H-1B employees can normally transfer to another job if the new employer files an H-1B petition within 30 days.

For more details on the H-1B, please consult an attorney or additional legal resources.

Because of the complex factors surrounding H-1B employment and life in the United States, there some additional, and possibly unexpected, things to consider. Here are some other important considerations when dealing with the H-1B or people holding it:

- It's very difficult for spouses of H-1B holders to get work authorization. Keep this in mind when considering an employee's personal situation—they're probably making a decision knowing they have to be the sole financial provider for their family. (At the time of this writing, regulations are pending that would grant employment authorization to some H-1B spouses.)

- Job security is possibly a higher priority, because it's required to continue residing in the United States.

- Once people have an H-1B, they're careful to protect it. They may be more risk-averse than your other employees and candidates.

Hiring Discussions

The unique circumstances of the H-1B visa mean that the process of hiring a good candidate—extending an offer, negotiating, aligning incentives, completing all of the paperwork—may surprise you if you're not familiar with it.

To start with, people who need this visa have a bit of a different mindset than, for example, a U.S. citizen, when it comes to employment offers. For example:

- They will often make decisions simply to maximize their chances of safely remaining in the country. This is completely rational, when you understand their perspective, but may surprise you if you don't. Offers that look superior in every other way might be declined because of this one consideration.

- After visa stability, they are probably focused next on the length of time to get their Green Card (become a permanent resident). If they're partway through the process with one company, they may prefer to continue there, even if the position is inferior to other opportunities. It also depends where they are in the process, and how much of a reset they're risking.

- When leaving the country, they will probably need to obtain a new visa entry stamp from a U.S. consulate. This can take a while, up to a few weeks, so vacations outside the country tend to be longer and less frequent.

Thousands of highly qualified professionals join U.S. companies every year on H-1B visas. Learning how the process works will help you recruit from this talent pool.

TN

Technically not a visa, TN status is a special program available to citizens of Canada and Mexico. Created as part of the North American Free Trade Agreement (NAFTA), it allows people in the United States, Canada, and Mexico to work in each North American country.

Applying for TN status is very similar to the process of obtaining a work visa such as the H-1B. It's a relatively straightforward process, but does require proof of employment (such as a job offer) before entering the United States. The TN visa has a couple important advantages over the H-1B:

- There's no annual limit.
- It can be extended indefinitely.
- It is faster. Canadian TN applications are submitted at the border or at an international airport in Canada, and are normally adjudicated within an hour. Mexicans can apply at a U.S. Consulate, a process that may take a week or two.

TN status is not transferable. If the holder wants to take a new job, they have to leave the country and restart the process.

E-3

Similar to the TN program and NAFTA, the E-3 visa was created as a result of the Australia-United States Free Trade Agreement (AUSFTA). It applies to Australian citizens with professional training and also has many advantages over the H-1B:

- Although it has an annual limit of 10,500 visas, this number has never been reached.

- It can be extended indefinitely.

- Spouses of E-3 holders may also work in the United States without restrictions.

- The application fees are low.

If done quickly, an E-3 holder can successfully transfer to a new job without returning to Australia.

F-1/OPT/STEM

The F-1 is one particular type of student visa that permits foreigners to study in America. It requires the recipient to have a full study schedule, and strictly limits the ability to work.

After graduation, however, F-1 holders can apply for Optional Practical Training (OPT), which permits them to stay in the United States to work for an additional 12 months. Although called "Training," OPT does not require a formal training program, and any employment qualifies, as long as it is in a field related to the employee's major field of study. The student will arrange for the OPT through the university, so there is zero burden on the employer in obtaining this form of work authorization. However, employees who join in F-1 OPT status will eventually need H-1B sponsorship.

Students in STEM fields (Science, Technology, Engineering, and Mathematics), which generally covers any prospective startup engineering hires, can extend this time by 17 more months, for a total of 29 months. This extension has important implications for subsequently obtaining an H-1B to remain in the United States, which we'll discuss in the next section.

J-1

The J-1 visa is designed to foster cultural exchange between countries. It can be used to support study or work abroad programs, so it may be useful in hiring people for limited amounts of time, such as work internships or co-ops. A formal training program, with milestones and educational goals, is usually required, and there are requirements for providing cultural enrichment. J-1 sponsors and employers are not permitted to use J-1 status as a temporary bridge while waiting for H-1B approval. Because of the administrative burdens and the short period of employment eligibility (usually one year for trainees), J-1 visas are usually not very cost-effective.

Green Card (Permanent Residence)

■ **Note** The U.S. Green Card program is complicated, takes many years to complete, and has many nuances. This section is only a rough overview, highlighting some of the important considerations for an employer.

A Green Card establishes a person's permanent residence in the United States. For employment purposes, a Green Card holder can work and move between jobs in the same way as a U.S. citizen. For people who want to have a long career working in the United States, attaining a Green Card is a tremendous relief, as they finally feel in control of their own destiny.

There are several ways to get a Green Card, but here we focus on the employer sponsorship. The application process is much longer, more involved, and more expensive than most work visas, but the value to the recipient is tremendous. You should at least consider participating for people you value and want to retain for a long time.

Green Card sponsorship can be a valuable short-term retention tool, since if you do not provide the sponsorship, the employee will leave for an employer who will. However, it cannot, in and of itself, be relied upon for long-term employee retention. If that's the only reason to stay, an employee will leave as soon as he or she gets the Green Card. As with U.S. citizens, salary, career advancement, and working conditions should be the primary retention tools, and the Green Card sponsorship can be considered a bonus.

The Process

There are two primary milestones for the Green Card application process.

Labor Certification (PERM)

The first step is typically to file a labor certification application with the Program Electronic Review Management (PERM) system. This requires demonstrating that there are not sufficient U.S. workers to fill the position, after conducting recruitment of U.S. workers pursuant to Department of Labor rules. A normal PERM case should take less than a year to complete, but some cases are selected for audit or additional processing, which can add a year. This is a tricky process, and as with all visa matters, should be led by an attorney who specializes in the field.

The PERM application also establishes the employee's *priority date*, which is very important, as it dictates when the Green Card application will finally be processed, years later. The applicant will want to ensure they preserve their priority date throughout their employment.

Immigrant Petition (I-140)

Once labor certification is approved, an employer can file form I-140 for employment-based immigration. The approved I-140 fixes the priority date, which the employee retains even after transferring to another employer.

Normally, an employee who was not born in India or China can obtain the Green Card a few months after the I-140 approval. However, the immigrant visas are allocated by country, and the quota for those born in India or China is oversubscribed.

At the time of this writing, the current backlog of applications for those born in India with Bachelor's degrees is approximately 13 years. Applicants with advanced degrees (such as a Masters or PhD), or who have jobs that require at least five years of experience, can file in a separate category, where the backlog is currently a mere eight years. This time is estimated from the priority date, which is why it's important to establish that date as early as possible.

It's possible, perhaps even likely, that legislative changes, court decisions, or executive actions will affect this process and the amount of time it takes. Immigration is a hot political issue in the United States, and there are many factors at work. It's wise to monitor the situation for new developments.

Costs

The total cost of a Green Card application depends on many details, but a rough estimate is around $10,000. It's important to note, however, that the first stage, labor certification, must be fully covered by the employer, and you're not allowed to seek reimbursement for it. This is one of the reasons that companies choose to wait some period of time (typically six months or one year) of employment before starting the process.)

H-1B Ramifications

A very important feature of the Green Card process is that it allows the employee to extend an H-1B visa beyond the typical six-year limit. There are two ways:

- If labor certification (PERM) has been completed at least one year before the end of the H-1B, it can be extended by one more year.

- If the I-140 petition has been approved at any time during the H-1B, it can be extended by three more years.

This is another reason that Green Card sponsorship is important for valued members of your team.

Successful Strategies

Now that you have some information, let's put it to use. These are strategies and other advice I've seen used successfully to hire people with work visas. It's not an exhaustive list, but should give you some ideas to get started.

Cover the Costs

You should plan, from the beginning, to cover all of the costs related to visa applications and attorney fees. In doing so, you remove a huge burden and source of anxiety from the candidate.

Start by finding an immigration attorney to work with on all of your company's cases. By creating a trusted relationship and amortizing the costs of each hire over time, you can leverage your investment into a much higher perceived value to prospective candidates, who face the daunting challenge of doing this alone.

Also, your competition is doing this already. For top candidates, this is simply table stakes.

Converting Graduates from F-1 to H-1B

Many international engineering students come to the United States to get a Masters degree, not only because of the high quality of graduate education, but also because it gives them a leg up on getting a work visa and, ultimately, a Green Card.

Most students are here on an F-1 visa, which only lasts as long as their education does. By extending their eligibility with F-1 OPT, plus the 17-month STEM extension, they can work for approximately 29 months after graduation. (Note: Membership in the government "E-Verify" program is required to get the STEM extension.)

While this extension is finite, it provides another benefit: The opportunity to apply for an H-1B two, or possibly three, more times. While the current lottery numbers indicate that a single application is likely to fail, being able to apply two or three times tips the odds in your favor. It's not a sure thing, but nothing in startup life is.

J-1 Work Exchange Programs

The J-1 visa, designed for work- or study-based exchange programs, is another option for hiring people for a limited period of time, especially interns. It requires that you consider a person's entire experience of working and living in the United States and provide some enrichment as part of it. Working in a startup can be a valuable experience, so it may be worth considering how to augment this in a way that makes the J-1 a good option. There are many organizations that can assist with program sponsorship.

Canadians Have an Advantage

TN status is much easier to obtain than an H-1B visa, meaning that Canadians (and, to some degree, Mexicans, although the rules are a bit different) are easier to hire than people from any other country. Furthermore, there's no limit or annual quota to worry about.

For practical purposes, it's pretty safe to think of hiring Canadian citizens in the same way that you would an American, except that it will take up to a few weeks to get all the paperwork prepared.

Summary of Visa Strategies

If there's one thing to take away from this discussion about visas, it's this: Find an immigration attorney. Having someone you can trust will open up many new hiring possibilities, and they will be indispensable as you grow your team.

And the first thing you should probably discuss with your attorney (and start thinking about now) is what your policy will be with respect to visa applications, and especially the Green Card, as you're likely to get asked about it and tested on your limits. For example: Will you offer Green Card sponsorship to everyone? Only to certain hires? If so, when are you willing to start the process? How much support will you give? And so on.

How do you find a good attorney? Consult your network. Other startup founders and hiring managers probably know somebody they've worked with and would recommend. Your Board of Directors will likely have some good referrals as well. Don't procrastinate this task just because you're not good friends with an immigration lawyer. Make it a top priority to find one.

Step #7: Develop Your Training Program

There's a common and tragic mistake made by many small companies and startups. They put lots of effort and resources into recruiting and hiring people with great potential, but that effort stops the day those people start work. It's an absolute shame to hire a great engineer, or someone who can become a great engineer, and not help them achieve their potential.

Before bringing in more new people, make sure you have a plan for onboarding. Facebook is famous for its six-week Bootcamp, a program that all new engineering hires must complete, no matter how much experience they already have.

Six weeks may be a bit much for a smaller company, but the main point is that you should at least have a *plan*. Consider including the following in your education for new hires:

- Describe the core principles of your company. What are the primary criteria you make to prioritize projects and judge their success?

- Show them your workflow—all the steps in the lifecycle of a project, from research and conception through to production deployment and verification.

- Work with them, possibly by pair programming with a senior team member, to complete a small project from beginning to end. This experience should give them a chance to learn and understand your workflow.

- Describe and outline the projects they'll be working on as they get started.

- Introduce their support structure. How and where can they find help? Of whom should they ask questions first?

At Course Hero, we recognized the need to create an onboarding process, as our new hires were having inconsistent results getting up to speed. We felt like we should be doing more to help them. So we put together an extremely simple, but ultimately effective, plan: Pair the new person with a senior engineer, until that senior engineer was confident the new hire was ready to work independently. The amount of time required, to cover all the points listed previously, depends on the experience of the new person, but in all cases we believe it's an excellent investment of our time.

Step #8: Find a Recruiter

Okay, now that you've considered the basics, let's throw some gas on the fire. If you're looking to hire rapidly, you're almost certainly going to need help from a recruiter.

The first mistake a lot of people make, when looking for a recruiter, is to assume they can just hand over the entire task to someone else.

Roll Up Your Sleeves

In his startup manifesto, "The Hard Thing about Hard Things," entrepreneur and venture capitalist Ben Horowitz writes that the best way to hire people into roles you don't understand is to try to do the job yourself:

> The very best way to know what you want is to act in the role. Not just in title, but in real action—run the team meeting, hold one-on-ones with the staff, set objectives, etc. In my career, I've been acting VP of HR, CFO, and VP of Sales. Often CEOs resist acting in functional roles, because they worry that they lack the appropriate knowledge. This worry is precisely why you should act—to get the appropriate knowledge. In fact, acting is really the only way to get all of the knowledge that you need to make the hire, because you are looking for the right executive for your company today, not a generic executive.

I believe the same applies to recruiting. For the best long-term results, you need to be willing to dive into recruiting directly, learning what works and what doesn't. Before you hire a recruiter, spend a month trying figure it out yourself. Then, when you do hire someone, you'll have a much better idea what's going to work.

Stay Involved

Even the best recruiters can't guess exactly which people are going to be right for your roles. They'll need to work with you, over time, to refine the search and match your expectations.

If the extent of your relationship with a recruiter is simply to receive incoming candidates, you're going to be dealing with a lot of noise in the channel. You should expect to maintain close contact with your recruiter, providing feedback about what's working and how to refine the search.

Look at this way, instead:

Once you've figured out what recruiting strategies and criteria are working for you (by rolling up your sleeves), hire a recruiter who lets you scale that effort up. You're trying to replicate and improve your technique by getting other people involved.

If you feel like the time you spend talking to a recruiter isn't being leveraged valuably into better results, you need to find a better recruiter.

Characteristics of Great Recruiters

You should consider a recruiter an essential and integral part of your team.

One of the fundamental problems with contingency-based recruiters is that their incentives aren't truly aligned with yours. By tying all of their compensation to the single act of getting an offer accepted, you're encouraging them to make choices that aren't optimal for you. They don't have a strong incentive to set your team up for long-term hiring success, nor do they benefit much by filtering out marginal candidates.

There's a better way. Find a recruiter who can help carry out (and improve) the hiring strategy you've already developed, and then simply pay them for their time. In the short-term, this means on an hourly, weekly, or monthly basis. In the long-term, this means hiring them as a full-time in-house recruiter.

But, you might be asking, doesn't this mean I could spend a lot on recruiting without getting any results? Of course. But most professionals, especially in highly-skilled fields, work this way. Start thinking about technical recruiting as a skill that requires years of experience to master, and maybe it will make more sense.

A great recruiter should also be able to help you with many other parts of the process as well, such as hiring discussions, negotiations, and crafting great job descriptions. Hiring recruiters on a contingency basis marginalizes their skills and the value they can provide to you and your team.

How to Find a Recruiter

Ask around. Who are the people and companies you know that have built teams quickly and effectively? Chances are, they had some help.

The best recruiters you find might all be booked already. That's ok—stay in touch with them. It's a fickle and cyclical business, so they might free up sooner than expected.

Finally, as discussed above, look for recruiters who prefer to work on a contract or hourly basis, not contingencies. They'll be confident they can deliver results, and not have you second-guessing their fees. In the long run, you'll save time and money, and get better hiring results, by working this way.

Step #9: Establish Long-Term Solutions

If you've created your recruiting pipelines, set up an onboarding program, crafted great job descriptions and company profile material, and found recruiters and immigration experts to help you, you're well on your way. You've done everything you can to achieve short-term results.

To continue building your team over several years, however, you should consider new initiatives. These things take longer to pay off, but will end up costing less, per hire, than what we've discussed so far. They will also help build engineering culture in your team, encouraging personal development among the people you already have.

Internships

Hiring engineering interns for your team, whether in the summer or any other time of year, can produce many benefits:

- Accomplishing additional projects
- Injecting fresh ideas or new concepts currently being taught in higher education
- Possible full-time hires upon graduation
- Building brand recognition for your company when they return to campus

An intern with previous work experience, strong academic credentials, and a good cultural match for your team can produce at the same level of a new hire, although only for a limited time. Less experienced or skilled interns will require more mentorship, but still can be a net positive. Beyond simply work product, though, interns can be a positive influence in many ways.

In terms of hiring, the competition for top students in college has extended back into the internships they complete during school. Even as their senior year begins, some of these students will already be "off the market," having accepted offers to return to the company where they spent the summer. The big players, such as Facebook and Google, will do everything they can to lock these students down before you even have a chance to talk with them. Therefore, if you want to compete, you'll need to get started even earlier.

Finally, having interns return to their school after a great experience with your company is a fantastic way to build interest in other students. It's a positive feedback loop—these students tell others, who apply the next year, who then continue spreading the word about your exciting, growing company.

Co-Ops

Similar to an internship, an increasing number of schools offer Co-operative education programs (or "co-ops"). Typically, co-ops are longer than internships and more central to the degree program of the school. Some degrees require co-op experience as a way of developing true work experience during a student's education.

Participation in a co-op program will require more effort on your part, as the school will want to ensure that its students are getting valuable experience. This investment can be well worth it, as the students produced by these programs tend to be more professionally prepared and capable.

One school that particularly stands out for its co-op program is the University of Waterloo in Waterloo, Canada. By the time students complete their degree, they will have done several extended internships, and tend to be well above average in both skills and readiness to enter the workforce. The secret is out, however—competition for top students at Waterloo is fierce, and the school has a huge staff dedicated to supporting this program.

Open Source Projects

Another option for building the attractiveness of your company in the long term is to create and contribute to open source software projects. This works in a few ways:

- People outside your company may find your software useful, and over time develop a good impression of you. Perhaps in the future they may even think, "That's a place I'd like to work."

- You and your engineers can start to build relationships with engineers outside the company. Not only can you learn from each other, but they may start to develop an interest in working with you more directly.

- Open source projects give people on your team a chance to show their work to the outside world. Most software engineering is anonymous, and many engineers are grateful and proud to have the chance to show some of their accomplishments to their friends and others.

It can take a while, but it's never too soon to start building an open source library to generate interest from the outside world and pride from your team.

Community Involvement

You can also build long-term benefits by becoming more involved in developer communities. The reasons are similar to those for open source projects. In particular, you have the opportunity to build relationships with engineers and technical people outside your company.

Some people are reluctant to encourage these types of activities, as they see it the other way around. The worry that by exposing their engineers to others, they run the risk of having them recruited away. I believe that this line of thinking is cynical and short-sighted.

You should believe that if an engineer from your company meets an engineer from another company, you're more likely to attract the other person to you, than vice versa. If this isn't true, then *stop worrying about recruiting and fix that problem*.

Summary

Recruiting is difficult, but it doesn't have to be mysterious. It's actually closer to science than it is to art. By committing yourself to diligent, thorough work, and by following industry-tested techniques, you can achieve success where many have struggled.

Hiring

Hiring Is Hard

You would like every hiring decision to be a slam dunk. In an ideal scenario, everyone on your team is enthusiastic about a candidate, the candidate is equally excited about your company, and it's just a matter of drawing up an offer and scribbling some signatures.

It rarely works out that way.

In the real world, building consensus on a hiring strategy is challenging, decisions are rarely unanimous, candidates are cagey and capricious, and sure things turn out to be anything but.

Furthermore, as a hiring manager, you're trying to make a two-sided sale: you need your own team to be supportive of the hiring decision, as well as convince the candidate that this is the right choice for them.

Let's discuss some of the trickiest parts of making a successful hire, and what you can do about them.

Agreeing on a Strategy

One of the most important aspects of your interview strategy is that each interviewer knows what they're looking for, and how to determine whether they've found it. They also need to trust that the composition of these interviews will give your team a complete picture, from which you can make a good decision.

It's critical to derive this strategy ahead of time. Once you're in a hiring meeting, it's too late. You have only the information you've gathered, so make sure it's useful. Calling back the candidate for additional interviews will instill doubts, and should be done only when absolutely necessary.

Chapter 3 listed a few valuable attributes to look for in software candidates. Once you've identified your own set of criteria, you need to devise the interview questions that will help you assess them, as well as any other job skills you require. For example, an interview plan (or at least part of it) for a back-end web developer might look something like this:

Technical interview: Algorithms and computer science fundamentals

In this interview, you'll want to assess the basic mathematical skills and logic that are essential to being an effective developer. You may also, however, want to find out how well the candidate can learn unfamiliar concepts and quickly develop an understanding of them. Perhaps they couldn't reverse a linked list right away. But after the interview, do you feel confident they could do it now?

Technical interview: Database design and practical skills

Similar to the first interview, you're looking to understand this person's ability to create and interact with a database. In addition, you could be looking to test their ability to find information to solve new problems. Given an unfamiliar task and access to Google, are they able to make good progress?

Product management interview

Talk to the candidate about how they view your product. How thoroughly do they understand it, and how much effort have they made? Do they have any ideas to make it better? In general, is this person going to help your company innovate, or would they prefer to simply code to someone else's spec?

Technical interview: Database design and practical skills

Similar to the first interview, in this session you're looking to understand this person's ability to create and interact with a database. In addition, you could be looking to test their ability to find information to solve new problems. Given an unfamiliar task and access to Google, are they able to make good progress?

And so forth. Throughout all of these interviews, you should be looking for signs of a cultural fit, and developing confidence that your team will enjoy working with this person.

It's also useful to look at whether the candidate applied information or discussions from earlier in the day to subsequent interviews. Did they keep making the same mistakes? Or were they paying attention, and showed that they can pick things up quickly and make use of them?

Getting to "Yes"

It's almost always easier to decide No on a candidate than Yes. It's the safe choice. It doesn't disturb your status quo, and doesn't create the risk of making a bad decision and dealing with the consequences. Furthermore, nobody's perfect, so there will always be something you can find for criticism.

As much as you would like your hiring decisions to be unanimous and straight-forward, it just doesn't happen that often. Even if someone is outstanding technically, there might be concerns about their enthusiasm for your company. On the other hand, someone might be a perfect cultural fit, but have some question marks in, for example, problem-solving ability.

One of the most important, and trickiest, skills you can develop as a manager (in a small company) is knowing how to guide your team toward the right decision. You should not be looking to make a unilateral decision, but rather to encourage the proper discussion that helps your team see candidates in the best light. And clearly, you need to know when to back off, when it's just not headed the right way.

In general, this means

- Preventing discussions from deep-ending on negative topics

- Considering the big picture—what will it mean to have hired this person, 3, 6, or 12 months from now?

- Detecting cynicism when it creeps into your team, and changing things up appropriately

- Making sure your interview process is gathering the correct information

Chapter 6 covers specific questions and discussion topics that will help you achieve consensus in hiring meetings.

Candidates Are Crafty

Once your team is a Yes on a candidate, you can shift into all-out sell mode. Focus all of your available attention on the candidate, and make closing the deal your top priority. Getting to this point took a long time, a team-wide effort, and a lot of false starts, so don't shortchange this part of the process. Here are some strategies and techniques for sealing the deal.

Keep Moving Fast

As with all parts of the hiring process, speed is critical. Your responsiveness and expeditiousness are keenly observed by candidates, and can strongly affect their impression of your team.

Getting an offer out quickly can absolutely improve your chances of having it accepted. Perhaps the chances increase only a small amount, but you're looking for any edge you can find.

Once the offer is out, your job isn't done. You need to stay in close contact with the candidate all the way until they make a decision. How often should you communicate? In my experience, once a day provides the right balance of demonstrating commitment without scaring people away.

Other ways you can keep moving fast:

- Answer questions immediately.

- Provide any necessary revisions as quickly as possible.

- Update the candidate on all the great things happening with your team, just during the time in which they're making a decision.

Finally, one of the most important reasons to be quick and responsive at all stages of hiring is that you can more realistically expect the same from the candidate. This can be *very* important.

How Tight Should Your Deadline Be?

The quicker your offer gets a response, the more likely that response is positive. Conversely, the longer it takes for a candidate to decide on your offer, the more likely they'll decline.

Therefore, you have an incentive to push for a quick decision. Push too hard, however, and you risk losing the candidate by making them feel uncomfortable or rushed.

Here's where your expediency throughout the hiring process is valuable. When you are quick and responsive at every stage, the urgency to accept an offer is much more authentic. If your team has taken five weeks to get through its interviews, an offer deadline of 48 hours is downright obnoxious. It suggests you don't value or respect the candidate's time. If, on the other hand, you've managed to get through everything in just a few days, and have consistently answered questions within an hour or two, it doesn't seem so crazy. You make things happen, and the candidate gets that.

So, how much time should give them to decide? If you've been quick through the process—and you should have been—two business days isn't unreasonable.

What if they ask for more time? I'll say this: *In all my years of hiring, I can't recall an instance where giving a candidate more time to consider an offer led to an acceptance.*

My preferred approach, when a candidate asks for more time to consider an offer, is to respond by asking what additional information would help them make a decision. (And then to make sure they get that information right away.) If they're waiting for other offers, learn as much as you can about those offers, and in particular the ways in which they're better than yours.

Another way to head this off is to ask the candidate about their timeline at the beginning of the process. If they indicate they've already planned to interview for a few weeks, consider delaying your interviews with them until they're closer to the end of that period. You want to engage the candidate when they're ready to act, so your impression is fresh and you can maintain positive momentum.

Finally, be up-front about your desire to get a quick response, so it doesn't come as an unwelcome surprise at the end of a promising discussion.

Negotiate Effectively

Hiring managers can benefit greatly from studying the art of negotiation, but be careful; hiring someone isn't like selling a car. In most sales situations, the relationship ends there. With hiring, however, you're creating a relationship that will (hopefully) last for many years. You're going to see and work with this person every day.

Talk to the candidate to find out their true decision points. It may take a while, but it's worth it, as their top criteria may not be what you think. A lot of people are motivated to find the highest possible salary—but not everyone.

At Course Hero, I was once about to lose a candidate to another startup. It wasn't quite a done deal yet, so I tried to learn why our offer didn't stack up. Was it money? No, that was competitive. Our product? No, education technology was appealing. Our team? No, the candidate would enjoy working with us and thought everyone was friendly. Only after ruling out these possibilities, and many others, was I able to uncover the crucial item: This person wanted to work on technically challenging problems, in order to develop, academically, as a computer scientist. After setting up a conversation with one of our engineers to go over some of our machine learning research, the candidate felt more comfortable about the opportunity, and joined us soon after.

You may not get every candidate, but don't rest until you at least know why.

For further study of negotiation, here are two recommended books:

- *Getting to Yes: Negotiating Agreement Without Giving In*, by Roger Fisher, William L. Ury, and Bruce Patton.[1]
- *Secrets of Power Negotiating: Inside Secrets from a Master Negotiator*, by Roger Dawson.[2]

Have No Regrets

Athletes talk about "leaving it all on the playing field." Not to push a sports metaphor too far, but I think the same applies to hiring.

In hiring, as in most negotiations, it's tempting to strive for the best "deal"— to hire somebody for the least cost possible. This feels like "winning" the negotiation.

I think this is a risky way to play it, and that the best approach starts with figuring out what your absolute best offer is. Hiring is too critical to whittle away at the margins. Get the right people in, as long as you can afford it. You're building the foundation of your company's future.

You don't have to put everything in the first offer. Sometimes you can tell that a round or two of revisions is likely, such as when the candidate informs you they have other offers. But have your best offer in mind and be prepared to give it. It's not a question of *if* you make your best offer, but *when*.

Set aside any regrets that you may have overpaid, and replace them with optimism that this new employee will exceed all of your expectations.

Hire at the Limit

Hopefully, you're always trying to hire people who make your team better. If so, you're constantly pushing the limits of the caliber of candidate you can successfully hire, which in turn means that the candidates you like are going to be a tough sell.

Don't be afraid and don't get discouraged. Aim high and do everything you can.

---

[1]Fisher, Roger, William Ury, and Bruce Patton, *Getting to Yes: Negotiating Agreement Without Giving In*. New York: Penguin, 2011.
[2]Roger Dawson, *Secrets of Power Negotiating: Inside Secrets from a Master Negotiator*. Pompton Plains, NJ: Career, 2011.

Your Job Doesn't End with the Offer

You've gotten the idea by now that your work does not end when you send an offer. You need to stay in close contact with candidates until they make a final decision.

Build a Connection

Once you decide that a candidate should be part of your team, consider ways to help them see what that would be like.

A great way to build a connection with a candidate is to set up an informal conversation with someone on the team. The two of them can discuss the day-to-day details of how you do things, what projects are going on, and answer any questions the candidate may not have been able to ask in an interview. If possible, choose someone who came into the company via a similar process—relocating from the same area, for example, or a graduate from the same school—to make the candidate even more comfortable with the idea of joining your team.

Another option is to invite the candidate to join your team for a work or informal activity. For example:

- Observe (or even participate in) a product meeting, to see what projects are active and how decisions get made. (Obviously, be careful about sharing confidential information.)

- Join your team for lunch, to see how friendly and welcoming you are.

- Participate in a team off-site activity, to start building relationships with others on the team.

The better a candidate gets to know you, the more they'll be able to visualize life in your company, which will only help them feel comfortable accepting an offer.

Connect with Students

Building a connection with college graduate hires is especially important. Students are unique in that they typically take longer, and interview with more companies, than other candidates. They also tend to be less sure about what they're looking for, and enthusiastic to just get started and see what they like.

The techniques listed previously work well with students, but may require more time and effort. Introducing a student to recent graduates on your team is helpful and effective. And once an offer is accepted, don't stop there—stay in touch and try to create a bond, so that their excitement builds as they finish their studies.

Start Preparing

Even before your candidate accepts an offer, it's not too soon to start preparing for them to join your team. Great people want to hit the ground running, and by discussing these topics, you'll get a better idea of how truly interested this person is in your company. Enthusiastic candidates will be excited to talk about these details, whereas candidates who aren't likely to sign will become quiet.

Here are a few specific ways to prepare:

- Ask the candidate for a start date. This question makes the decision very real, if it wasn't already. It also gives you an idea of how much time you have to get ready.

- Ask the candidate what kind of tools they need or want. What kind of laptop? Would they like any additional hardware? Get them to start envisioning their dream setup—in your office.

- Some candidates will ask what they can do to prepare. If this happens, be ready to respond with some ideas. This is a great way to get them more engaged.

- In some cases, and with the candidate's permission, it's helpful to introduce them to some or all of your team. They may want to learn more about how you do things, get advice on their upcoming job transition, or ask questions about the company.

The more you can get a candidate to think and act as part of your team, the easier you make it for them to join in earnest.

Summary

The final stages of the hiring process are the toughest, full of a variety of pitfalls as you try to successfully convince great candidates to join your team. By crafting a realistic and effective strategy, learning how to negotiate, and seeing things through all the way until an employee's first day on the job, you may not guarantee success, but you can at least tip the odds a bit more in your favor.

The Myth of the Ninja Rockstar Developer

In 2007, I was hired as a senior web developer at the local events search engine Zvents. On my first day, not more than 15 minutes after entering the office as an employee for the first time, the CEO asked me, "Are you our new rockstar developer?"

To be clear, he meant well. He meant the term as a compliment, consistent with industry jargon, as well as an expectation of big things.

I had certainly heard the term before, but was still taken aback. I had never thought of myself as a "rockstar" before, and wasn't entirely sure what it truly meant. (Actually, it might be more accurate to say I already thought of myself as a failed rockstar, having played keyboard in a few rock bands in my younger days, none of which achieved the glory we had hoped.)

I don't recall exactly how I responded to the CEO, but I definitely tried to create a more accurate and professional expectation of what I could do. To be called a rockstar was flattering, in a way, but not something with which I felt totally comfortable.

Where Did All These Ninjas and Rockstars Come From?

For reasons I don't completely understand, a certain vernacular has taken over the description of talented software engineers. It's no longer good enough to simply be an excellent engineer, now people have to be ninjas or rockstars.

Figure 6-1 shows the growth of the term "ninja" over the past six years. The term appears to originate, or at least first appear widely in technology culture, with John Resig's book, *Secrets of the JavaScript Ninja*.[1] Resig, one of the most widely-respected authors on software development, and now Dean of Computer Science at Khan Academy, had noble intentions for the use of this term. From the book's description:

> *You can't always attack software head-on. Sometimes you come at it sideways or sneak up from behind. You need to master an arsenal of tools and know every stealthy trick. You have to be a ninja.*

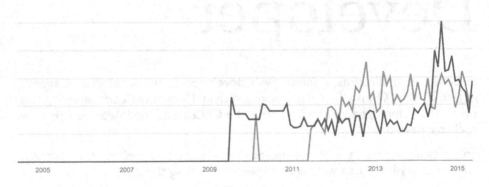

Figure 6-1. Google trends for the terms "python ninja" (Blue) and "ruby ninja" (Red)[2]

Unfortunately, usage of the term "ninja" has gone a bit sideways since then, with developers everywhere referring to themselves as ninjas and companies trying desperately to hire ninjas for everything from software development to human resources. Figure 6-2 shows a sample of listings returned by searching LinkedIn Jobs for "ninja."

[1] Resig, John, and Bear Bibeault. *Secrets of the JavaScript Ninja*. Manning Publications, 2013.
[2] https://www.google.com/trends/.

Customer Service Representative (**Ninja**)
Sixthman
Greater Atlanta Area • May 28, 2015
Similar

UI/UX Designer (Design **Ninja**)
BitGo
Palo Alto, CA, US • May 11, 2015 • From workable.com
Similar

Paid Search (PPC) **Ninja** wannabe – 90 days
Internship with a Full-time opportunity
Sellpoints
Emeryville, CA, US • May 31, 2015 • From www.smartrecruiters.com
Similar

Firmware **Ninja**
Qvivr
Sunnyvale, CA, US • May 29, 2015 • From track.zipalerts.com
Similar

Figure 6-2. Some of the top hits for the search "ninja" on LinkedIn Jobs[3]

The history of "rockstar" as it pertains to software development is a bit harder to trace, but probably less benign. Referring to anyone as a rockstar connotes a type of behavior that doesn't always fit well in a team dynamic—brilliant, but high-maintenance; productive, but seeking individual glory.

There are other theories on the use of these terms as well. Some people believe that they're used as a cheap appeal to one's ego. Lauding a developer with honorifics may reduce their requirements in terms of actual influence or even compensation. This is certainly a cynical interpretation, and in most cases, such an effect would be short-lived.

Similarly, the language around rockstars and ninjas may reflect an attempt to make software development more cool or fashionable. As the profession has become more central to our modern economy, there's a growing need to attract and retain those who are skilled at it. You could argue we need more people to aspire to be rockstar developers than, well, actual rockstars.

What's the Big Deal?

Okay, so maybe a few engineers or other startup folks are feeding their egos by being called rockstars or ninjas. Whom is this really hurting?

It's hurting you, the person trying to build a team. Here's why:

- *It creates a false expectation of someone's ability or potential for impact.* Rockstars—actual rockstars—capture the hearts of millions, bring in tons of money, and affect the culture of an entire society. (They also tend to trash hotel rooms and flame out quickly.) It's not accurate or even fair to suggest the next developer you hire is going to have an impact on that scale. It's setting you and the developer up for disappointment.

- *These people don't really exist.* Rockstars are literally one in a million, or even fewer, and ninjas have barely existed outside mythology for hundreds of years. It may be difficult to find a software developer, but the odds are still orders of magnitude better than one in a million. These terms create a false feeling of scarcity, further feeding the preconception that you can only hire truly exceptional candidates—mythical characters who don't actually exist. Developers, by contrast, do exist, and deserve your attention and consideration.

- *These terms artificially elevate people out of proportion to their contributions, which can damage your company culture of trust and collaboration.*

- *People who truly act like rockstars and ninjas might not be the best for your team.* Remember, rockstars are known for their flamboyant disregard for the property and feelings of others, and ninjas, well, they kill people. Even if your people don't internalize these characteristics to the extreme, it's still a message that can be counterproductive.

- *You're trying to assemble a team.* Even the most successful rock bands have how many stars—one, maybe two? The Beatles and The Rolling Stones, arguably the two most influential and successful bands of all time, were unique in the way all of their members became stars in their own right, but even in these cases, there were only four such people. At the time of this writing, Course Hero's Engineering and Design team has 28 people, and I can't think of any rock bands with 28 identifiable star personalities.

It may seem harmless, but indiscriminate use of the terms "rockstar," "ninja," and others like them can undermine your efforts to build a quality software engineering team.

Better Terminology for Software Developers

Hopefully you're now convinced that you shouldn't call your developers "rockstars" or "ninjas." But what should you call them instead?

Most developers, especially the ones you want to hire, are perfectly content with a description that matches what they actually do, such as "Senior Software Engineer," "Mobile Developer," or "UX/UI Designer." Keep it simple and you'll be fine. This will also make it easier to have an open conversation about the expectations of the role and the things on which it's important to focus.

Summary

The high-stakes environment of Silicon Valley has, for many years, built up the premise that you must find the absolute best, the most elite technical minds of the world, in order to succeed. This emphasis on finding exceptional developers has contributed to a culture and vocabulary in which it's not enough to hire someone proficient or competent—they need to be "rockstars" or "ninjas." Not only is this terminology arbitrary and elitist, it's not even accurate.

For the best results building your technical team, stop thinking about mythical characters and spend your time focused on people who actually exist.

The Hiring Decision Checklist

Startups experiencing rapid growth have a lot of hiring meetings. In fact, these meetings may be the single largest use of meeting time in your company.

In my early days at Course Hero, hiring meetings tended to be long, drawn-out discussions that often went in circles. We debated topics that were often too open-ended and general to be useful. For example:

- Is this person smart?
- Do they match our requirements?
- Do they fit in with the culture?

At the end of the meeting, we had a hard time making clear, confident decisions.

Over time, we've refined our discussions to be much more efficient and decisive, and one of the biggest improvements has been to articulate a specific, actionable checklist of characteristics to discuss:

- What is this person's ceiling?
- How does this person make us better?
- Is this person teachable?

- What exactly will this person work on during the first 30/90 days?
- Will we like being around this person?

We don't always discuss every item for every candidate. Knowing which ones to focus on with each candidate is an important skill that you and your team will learn over time.

Let's discuss each question in more detail.

What Is this Person's Ceiling?

Growing companies are looking for people who have a lot of potential. As a leader in such a company, you need and expect people to expand into new positions with the company, take on bigger challenges, and generally unlock new skills and talents. You want each new hire to be a great long-term addition, not just fill a short-term need.

Senior candidates are probably closer to their ceiling already, which should come through in the form of strong job skills. But in every case, we want to find someone with the potential to be outstanding. If you look forward, beyond where this person's skills are right now, what do you see?

The definition of "ceiling" depends on your company, role, and culture. In general, however, you might want to:

- Compare the role you're considering for the candidate to one that's more senior. For example, for a junior engineer, this might be a senior engineering role. Are you confident this person will be able to hold that role someday?

- Consider whether the candidate has shown a consistent track record of improvement and learning throughout their career. Does that growth or learning appear to have tapered off or hit a plateau?

- Consider how quickly and enthusiastically this person can learn new things. (More on this in a bit.)

It's worth spending time to decide how your team evaluates someone's ceiling, in order to make these discussions more productive.

How Does this Person Make Us Better?

It's far easier to find reasons why you shouldn't hire someone than make a convincing case that you should, especially when one negative opinion has veto power. I've found it helpful to flip the question around and ask the team to look for specific ways this person will improve our team. For example:

- What skills do they have that we don't?
- What can they do better than anyone here?
- What can they teach us?
- What changes to our culture or process will they lead or precipitate to make us better?

With junior candidates, it might be less obvious, but there should still be some potential. For example, will their creativity help us brainstorm new projects? Will their ambition drive us to accomplish more? Will they bring in new, fresh ideas?

If you can't come up with at least one specific way that a potential employee will improve your team, it's probably not a good match.

By contrast, if you find that you're learning new and useful things from the candidate during the interview, you've probably found a great addition to your team.

Is this Person Teachable?

For any hire, we're going to be investing precious time helping them succeed. For a junior hire, this means on-the-job technical training, mentorship, and patience as they learn the skills to be effective. For a senior hire, it means helping them understand our code base, practices, and philosophy, so that they can start contributing and improving what we do.

In all cases, we want to be confident that there's going to be a great return on that investment. For example:

- Will they learn something the first time, or will we have to keep reminding them?
- Will they be able to extrapolate new skills and ideas into problems they haven't seen before?
- Are they open-minded about how to do things?

In a growing company, it's also important to have people who can themselves grow—who can learn new things, take on new responsibilities, and solve the increasingly complex problems that your organization will face. Being teachable is a critical characteristic for achieving this personal growth.

What Will this Person Work On?

It's important to discuss the specific projects on which you anticipate a new hire will work during their first 30, 60, or 90 days. If this is difficult—if you can't come up with a good list of valuable tasks that you're confident they can handle—that's a bad sign.

Create a detailed roadmap of projects for this person and then ask the following questions:

- Is this work worth the cost of hiring someone?
- Will we be happy in 90 days with these results?
- What does this free other people on our team up to do?

This topic can bring a lot of clarity to the hiring discussion.

Will We Like Being Around this Person?

Sometimes called the "Airport Test," it's important to discuss how you'll feel about spending several hours per day with this person. You go through a lot of good and bad times as a team, and it's a lot easier to do so with people who generally make you happy.

One way to help assess this quality in candidates is to include interview questions that test self-awareness and emotional intelligence. For example:

- Tell me about a time when a project went off track. How did you know, what did you do, and what did you learn from the experience?
- What do you enjoy about your work?
- How will this position help you achieve what you want?

People with high emotional intelligence—who understand how their actions affect those around them—are likely to be great teammates and generally pleasant people with whom to spend several hours solving hard problems each day.

Summary

At Course Hero, we've managed to cut our hiring meetings from an average length of one hour down to about 15 minutes. This is a valuable savings, since we're doing more hiring than ever. We've also adjusted our interview approach to make sure we get answers to these five hiring questions.

The specific questions you use may be specific to your team, but answering these types of questions, as a team, will help focus your hiring decisions.

Making Interviews Fun for Your Team

Interviews should be fun. Think about it... You get to meet people, learn new things, and hear about interesting experiences. Why wouldn't it be an enjoyable experience?

Unfortunately, the interview process in many companies is mundane, mechanical, and, frankly, joyless. Conducting interviews is considered just another obligation that contributes to an engineer's "overhead"—time spent doing things less fun than building a product.

You'll get the best results if your team truly enjoys conducting interviews. They'll be more enthusiastic, more engaged, and more insightful. Candidates will notice the attitudes of your interviewers as well, and they will respond positively to a team that appears to love their work. This perception can be critical for landing the best hires.

Finally, some personalities are simply better suited to being an interviewer. Look to build a team that possesses, in addition to the necessary technical and analytical skills, the ability to connect with people, a deep empathy for others, and consistent enthusiasm for your company and their work.

The Importance of Fun Interviews

You may be thinking, "Isn't this kind of silly? Interviews are serious business and too important to worry about being fun." Actually, the importance of the interview is exactly why it should be fun for everyone involved.

Fun for the Candidate

You've probably heard that an interview is a two-way street—while you're interviewing a candidate, they're simultaneously sizing up you, your team, and the opportunity. Obviously, you want them to have a favorable impression of you, and one of the best ways to accomplish this goal is for them to enjoy their time with you. There are many ways to make an interview more enjoyable for the candidate. For example:

- Start with a tour of your office and the best benefits of working there. Sell them on your company from the very beginning. Candidates know they're going to get grilled, so taking the time to pitch them up front shows optimism that they'll do well, which can rub off on them.

- Give the candidate some goodies to take home, such as a company T-shirt or mug. Again, it's a sign of faith and confidence in their ability, which creates a positive impression.

- Bring candidates into team activities. Social events such as team lunches are a great way for a candidate to meet and learn about a lot of people in your company, not just the ones interviewing them. When possible, meetings about engineering design or product development are also highly engaging ways to help a candidate envision life in your company.

- Select and train interviewers to be engaging and personable. Your interview team is representing your company to the candidate—put your best foot forward.

- Compose your interviews of interesting and novel questions and challenges. If your interview questions are the same tired ones that candidates have been hearing for years, they won't think of you as a dynamic engineering team with a forward-thinking culture. Some of the best interview questions are derived from problems your team is actually facing. Such questions also give candidates a better picture of the work they might do at your company.

Every candidate who visits your office should come away hoping to work there. Resist the temptation to lower enthusiasm for candidates you know aren't going to succeed—keep selling until the very end. Look at it this way: A candidate who doesn't get an offer from you is going to be disappointed, of course, and probably going to be thinking one of two things:

- Eh, I didn't like that place anyway.
- Darn! That place is awesome.

You definitely want them thinking the latter, for several reasons:

- They may be more qualified in the future and worth considering again.
- They might recommend your company to friends or colleagues.
- A prospective candidate, upon hearing of their interview, may ask for their opinion of your team.

Every time a new person walks into your office, including job interviewees, you have an opportunity to sell and promote your company to the world. Take advantage of these opportunities, as you never know to what they may lead.

Fun for Your Team

An engineer who dreads interviewing candidates will look for excuses not to participate, provide feedback veiled in cynicism, and represent your company in an unfavorable light. It's critical to find ways to make the process enjoyable for your engineers, and a process in which they value being a part. Tolerating interviews isn't good enough—you want your team to look forward to them.

What makes an interview fun for an engineer?

Quality Candidates

First and foremost, the interviewee must be a high-quality candidate. Engineers are intellectually curious and creative people and enjoy talking with others who share these traits.

Some of the best interviews are those in which the interviewer feels like they learned something useful or important. This experience makes a strong impression that hiring the candidate will lead to lots more learning and growth.

By contrast, an interview with a poor candidate will feel like a waste of time. If this happens too many times, the engineer will start trying to figure out how to get out of the interviews altogether. Who could blame them?

In order to make sure your team is only spending time with high-potential candidates, perform rigorous screening at the start of the process. For most engineering positions, this will mean a focus on technical aspects of the job, particularly coding, as this tends to be the most difficult requirement to meet.

As a rule of thumb, aim for at least a 50% success rate for candidates in the next interview round. For example, once you've advanced a candidate to a full on-site interview, they should have at least even odds of getting a positive decision from your team. If you don't think a candidate's chances are that strong, you probably shouldn't invest any more time with your team.

A high success rate ensures that your interviewers will treat each new candidate with optimism and excitement. They'll be looking for good reasons to hire this person, rather than excuses not to.

An Example from Course Hero: Conduct Interviews in Reverse

Most teams start their interview process with an engineer. If that goes well, the candidate typically comes in for several more engineering interviews. And then, only after all the engineers have given a collective thumbs-up, does an executive or manager come in for the final assessment and possibly make an employment offer.

At Course Hero, we flip that around.

Our interviews start with me, the executive in charge of the engineering team. Here's why:

- I prefer to assume that an engineer's time is more valuable than mine. Even if that's not always true, the time of five or six engineers definitely is. It's better to lose an hour of my time than several hours, combined, from the team.

- I also want to make sure that our engineers generally have a good experience in their interviews, and it's a lot more fun to interview a great candidate. By making interviews something that the team looks forward to, we get the best results and collectively give the interview process the priority it deserves.

- Finally, this process helps me to keep thinking like an engineer. As my own job has progressed away from writing code on a daily basis, the regular interaction over code in our interviews helps me stay at least somewhat connected to the craft. It's usually the only time of the day I get to write any code, even if it's just pairing with the candidate.

I don't do the typical executive interview. This is mostly technical—after a few questions about the candidate's interest, motivation, and other details, we jump right into some coding and design. I want to be confident that anyone passing the interview has a good chance of succeeding with the rest of the process. We can always meet again to discuss high-level topics, if necessary.

Being the first interviewer also lets me start selling the candidate on Course Hero from the beginning. Interviewing is truly a two-way process, and if you do nothing but grill a candidate for several hours before discussing the merits of your company and the position, you risk pushing them away. A motivated candidate is probably going to perform better, and it's in your interest to have everyone trying their best.

Owning the Process

Your interview process is just as much a work product of your team as the code you write. If you don't practice top-down, waterfall project management for product development, you shouldn't apply that technique here either. Your interview team will do their best if they feel some personal ownership of the strategy and responsibility for the results.

One of the best ways to involve your team is to have them craft their own interview questions. The overall composition of the entire interview needs to carefully planned, but this can be done with a bottom-up approach. For example:

- Give each interviewer an area to test (for example, SQL and relational databases), but let them devise the actual questions.

- Encourage your engineers to derive their interview topics from real-world problems, so that the interview results are a good predictor of job performance.

- Construct and review the overall interview strategy with input from all members of your team.

- Discuss and review your list of hiring criteria and requirements with your team.

You'll know your team feels ownership of the process when they start to suggest unsolicited improvements or, even better, recruit candidates on their own.

How to Make Interviews Fun: Screen Out All But the Best Candidates

Interviewing engineers, like engineering work itself, is a creative process, and people perform better in creative roles when they're happy. How can you make interviews fun, overall?

For engineers, the most enjoyable interviews are generally conducted with high-caliber candidates. For example:

- It's satisfying to have someone solve problems effectively with you.
- You can start to imagine how much better your team will be with this person on board.
- You may learn new things during the interview.
- It's just generally fun to converse with a bright, friendly person.

Here's the key insight: If you screen out all but the very best candidates before your team even talks with them, you ensure that nearly every interview they conduct is going to be fun. Furthermore, as they learn that interviews are fun, they become more enthusiastic about participating, which leads to better interviews and a better representation of your team to the candidate.

Many teams share the load of screening candidates. It's certainly easy to see why—initial phone screens, resume reviews, and other early phases of the recruiting process are arduous, repetitive tasks. Under the weight of this responsibility, it's tempting to divide and conquer.

If at all possible, however, you, as the manager of a team of busy engineers, should try to shoulder this burden yourself. Sharing the difficult parts of recruiting and interviewing will just make everyone equally frustrated with the process. Your job is to make everyone else more productive, and ensuring that your engineers only interact with exciting, high-quality prospective new teammates is one of the single biggest ways you can do this.

Who Makes a Good Interviewer?

In general, it's good to involve as much of your team as possible in your interviews. Participation in the process and in the decision-making builds a sense of ownership and responsibility, which will help bring out the best in those taking part.

Not everyone is born to be an interviewer, however. One way to help make interviews fun for your team is to select interviewers who naturally enjoy the process. It's also important to select and trust the people on your team who perform the function well.

Here are some qualities to look for in your interview team.

Technical and Analytical Skill

Technical skill is probably the first thing teams and managers consider when selecting interviewers. It's not the only consideration, but it's certainly very important. In order to determine the breadth and depth of the candidate's skill, an interviewer needs to be at least as strong.

Don't forget: The candidate is testing you as well. Most engineers care deeply about the ability to learn from their colleagues, so they're looking to see if your team has the knowledge and skill to teach them new things.

Empathy for Others

Only people who actually have emotional intelligence can test for it in others. A growing body of research indicates that this type of intelligence—which includes self-awareness, the understanding of motivating factors, regulating one's own emotions, and empathy for others—is highly influential in individual and team success.

You may need to learn more about emotional intelligence yourself, so that you can identify it in your team. As with technical ability, this quality will be noticed and judged by your interview candidates. Just like you, they want to work with people who understand and care about them, and will be helpful allies as they confront difficult challenges.

Enthusiasm for Their Work

Not everyone loves their work, but you only want to hire people who do. For someone to be excited to join your team, and bring their energy and excitement to your company, they absolutely need to feel that this enthusiasm will be reciprocated.

Your interviewers, and in fact everyone in your company, should be selling a candidate on your company's merits at every opportunity. Even if they don't get the job, you want them to wish they had. They'll talk with friends and colleagues afterward—whether it's three days or three years—and you want their impression to be as positive as possible.

It's difficult to fake enthusiasm for something for an entire hour or more. Be sure that everyone on your interview team is truly excited about what they do and the opportunities ahead.

Summary

Conducting an interview is more than just asking questions and writing down the answers. It's a chance to connect with a new person, discuss interesting ideas, and make an important decision affecting the future of your company.

If people on your team, or the candidates you interview, don't seem to appreciate being part of this process, something's wrong. By planning an enjoyable experience for the candidate, aggressively screening out all but the best candidates early on, and sharing ownership and responsibility with your team, you can work toward a process that everyone enjoys and embraces, ultimately leading to better results.

Why We Don't Allow Java in Job Interviews

An engineering interview process should be designed to quickly and accurately select the best candidates. As each team is different, the requirements and criteria for hiring will vary. What's important, though, is that your process helps you increase your precision and make the best use of your time. Don't be afraid to challenge conventional wisdom or industry standards along the way.

At Course Hero, we've taken the very unusual step of removing Java, one of the most widely-used and widely-known programming languages in the world, from our coding interviews. It was a difficult decision to make, and one that we debated at length, but the results have been excellent.

Whether or not such a policy is right for you and your team, it is my hope that our experience will help you think of ways to examine and question traditional interviewing methods and discover more accurate predictors of success.

No Java

A few months after I joined Course Hero, we instituted an important, and somewhat unusual, change to our interview process.

We no longer allow candidates to use Java.

For all parts of the hiring process that involve writing code (which is most of them), candidates are free to choose any language they like. Except Java.

None of us, myself included, has any personal issue with Java as a programming language. It's unquestionably one of the most powerful, versatile, and influential languages ever devised. Like many software engineers, I've written countless programs and architected myriad applications, large and small, in Java.

Course Hero is an analytical company, and we're always looking at data for signs of improvements to be made. Hiring is no exception. After my first 40 or 50 phone screens at Course Hero, I was beginning to notice a pattern—candidates who chose Java for their interviews tended to fare poorly.

At this point, I wasn't looking for a reason why that might be the case. I just wondered if the data was trying to tell us something. I asked the other engineers who conduct interviews, and they said that now that I mentioned it, it seemed like a pattern for them as well.

We do a lot of interviewing, so I'm always looking for something that will help us separate signal from noise, and I was starting to think we were on to something. I next looked at our recent hiring history, to see what language had been chosen in those successful instances. Of the last 14 engineering hires, only two had used Java, and both people indicated another language would have been fine too. (The most frequently chosen languages were PHP and Python.)

Now we were really on to something. Java was almost never used by people we ended up hiring, and was frequently used by people who fared poorly. In coding interviews, we let the candidate choose the language, while keeping the questions or challenges the same. The candidate is also free to change languages at any time, so it's unlikely that Java is simply a poor match for our interview questions.

With this analysis, we were ready to cut Java out of the picture, but wanted to be thoughtful about how to best make this change. Since many of us still like programming in Java, we also discussed and debated why this poor performance could be happening.

What's Wrong with Java?

Why have we moved away from Java? This is really just a data-driven decision. Candidates who have chosen Java in our interviews have fared poorly, on average. And, of the ones who did well (and those who we subsequently hired), each person indicated they would have been just as comfortable in another language.

But this experience also got us thinking about why this phenomenon might be happening. Here are some possible explanations.

Java for Web Apps

Course Hero is a web startup, doing web development. For this type of work, Java is not as frequently the tool of choice for people using modern practices and methodologies. Exceptions exist, of course, but in many ways, languages such as Python, Ruby, PHP, and JavaScript are better suited for rapid development, iteration, and deployment of a consumer web product. Since this is the type of work we do, our interviews reflect and try to emulate these factors.

For example, some of our coding challenges require parsing and manipulating strings of text—common tasks when dealing with millions of user-generated text documents. Python, Ruby, and PHP have handy built-in methods that make these manipulations simple, whereas Java requires a bit more complicated approach.

Java Is Just One of Many Tools

For web development interview problems, Java is often not the best choice for creating a clear, concise solution. It's tough to watch someone write 20 lines of Java for something that can be done in one line of Python. Being aware of the capabilities of multiple languages and being able to select the right one for a particular task are important skills.

We're looking for candidates who can learn quickly and apply that learning to new problems. For this reason, we prefer to conduct the interview in a language well suited for our work, even if it's less familiar to the candidate, to see how well they can pick things up with our help. We frequently find that candidates prefer to use familiar techniques, especially in Java, even when they're not the best choice for a particular problem.

Furthermore, we're looking for candidates who try to stay current on the latest thinking and trends in web development. Languages such as Python and Ruby, as well as JavaScript frameworks like Node.js, AngularJS, and jQuery, have enjoyed a faster pace of innovation and experimentation in recent years. The technology industry changes quickly, and it's important to build a team of people who can change along with it. A desire to learn and play with new development tools correlates positively with strong performance in the rest of our interview process.

Side Projects

Another strong indicator of creativity and energy in a software engineer is the presence of side projects. Many of the best engineers I've worked with are constantly tinkering with new ideas or tools. They're looking for better, more powerful ways to build, and no responsible engineer would kick off a large project with an untested, unfamiliar technology. And in many cases, these side projects are done in new languages, as a way to learn.

I believe—and I know many will disagree—that you're less likely to find a creative, diligent, forward-looking engineer who has done side projects only in Java.

People Start with Java

Java is the most common language used in computer science instruction and has been for many years. Any computer science degree completed in the past 15 years likely included a lot of Java for projects and coursework. To succeed in a startup, however, you need the drive to learn new things and a wide variety of skills, and someone using only what they learned in class probably hasn't shown that drive yet. Startups need engineers who aren't satisfied with the basic skills that everyone is taught; they need explorers and creative, curious minds who are always looking for better ways to solve hard problems.

Classes focused on web development do tend to use a wider variety of languages, such as Python and Ruby. Students who have moved past the basics and begun to specialize in software engineering for the web are more likely to have skills in languages other than Java, and these are typically the students we're looking for.

Just because Java can be used for nearly anything doesn't mean it's the best choice for everything.

Results: Has this Policy Worked?

At the time of this writing, Course Hero's "No Java" policy has been in place for nearly a year. During this time, we've screened and interviewed hundreds of candidates. Here are some of our early findings.

Interviews Are More Focused

As mentioned, Java isn't a perfect fit for many of our interview questions. Working on solutions in Java is a bit more convoluted and makes it harder to see and discuss the important logic underlying the candidate's implementation.

By using a better-suited language, we're able to more quickly and consistently hone in the actual problem-solving ability of the candidate. Perhaps more importantly, we're more confident about our analysis of the interview and our ability to make decisions afterward. The results are more clear.

Sometimes We Give In

Occasionally, we relent. For a variety of reasons—for example, when the candidate pushes unusually hard to use Java, or the candidate is a new grad and has little experience outside Java—we sometimes give in and let a candidate proceed in Java.

We always regret it.

Seemingly without exception, the candidates for whom we allow Java fail to meet our expectations. They don't have the technical skill, creativity, or ability to learn quickly that we need.

Interestingly, many candidates who prefer Java end up doing better in another language. I recently conducted an interview with a young candidate who clearly preferred Java, but was a good sport and agreed to give it a try in C++ (his second choice). Although he was rusty, he showed a lot of good traits—he took suggestions well and made use of them, learned new concepts quickly, and came up with multiple approaches to hard problems. Halfway through the interview, it was painfully clear he was frustrated in C++, so I offered him the chance to switch to Java for the second half of the session. He gratefully accepted. Once in Java, however, he reverted to familiar habits, whether they were a good solution or not. He stopped listening as much to suggestions. He was less creative in looking for alternative solutions. In summary, he may have felt more comfortable, but his overall interview performance suffered noticeably.

Based on our results, we've become more insistent about the "No Java" rule.

Personality Screening

Restricting the use of Java has filtered out more than just technical skills. It has also helped us screen candidates who don't have the desire and capability to push themselves and learn new things.

To our initial surprise, people rarely raise a fuss when they learn they won't be able to use Java. Some are clearly anxious, but our experience so far is that they do just fine in the interview. Very few, however, are upset to the point where they lose interest in the opportunity. We often have an open discussion about the policy and why we believe it's important. Most people understand our goals and are happy to proceed. In the rare cases where somebody declines to continue, we're confident it wasn't going to be a good match, and if anything, we're grateful to have figured that out more quickly.

It's Awkward

There's no denying that carrying out this policy has been, at times, socially awkward. An interview may be off to a great start—developing a good relationship with the candidate, starting to understand the depth of their skills and experience, and feeling optimistic about their overall chances—when you have to throw in this unusual wrinkle. It's so unexpected that it typically takes people aback. The question is, for how long?

We have two basic choices when it comes to enacting the policy:

- Tell everyone about the No Java policy at the very beginning of the interview process, to prevent confusion when we get to coding interviews.

- Wait until it's time to write code and see what language the candidate chooses. Only if they choose Java will we have to discuss the policy.

We've decided to go with the first approach. We'd much rather clear up any confusion or concern early in the process, rather than during the most important part of the interview, when the candidate is about to showcase their coding skills.

No matter how you carry out a policy like this, there's going to be some social awkwardness. In order to have such a policy, you need to be willing to enforce and defend it in a variety of circumstances.

Summary

At Course Hero, we've made a somewhat unusual and controversial decision to exclude Java from our software engineering interviews. The results have been good for us so far, even if we can't fully explain why, or what it means.

Such a policy isn't necessarily right for you and your team, but don't be afraid to think differently. Everything about a startup should be considered for experimentation and innovation, including how and why you conduct your interviews.

One more note: We're definitely not suggesting people should stop learning Java! It's a powerful and useful language. What we are suggesting, though, is that if you're interested in fast-paced, modern web development, you should have a few more tools in your belt.

Managing

CHAPTER

10

Do I Want to Be a Manager?

Years ago, in an interview for an engineering management position, I was asked, "Why do you like being a manager?" I had never been asked this question so plainly. Having no prepared answer, I had to think about it for a bit. Finally, I responded, "I like to make people happy."

It's more than just making people happy, of course. A more complete description of technical management might be, "Achieving business and product objectives while simultaneously creating an engineering culture that delivers results and makes people feel their work has an impact and that they are progressing and developing new skills."

You'll struggle to be effective in the long run, however, if you don't truly enjoy the idea of making people happy. Not just your direct reports, but all of the other departments of the company that count on you as well—Product, Marketing, Support, and so on. All of these people are looking to you to make them more productive, efficient, confident, and, well, *happy*.

As you consider the prospect of a career managing engineers, let's discuss some of the important aspects of the role.

You Work for Them

Contrary to what you may see and hear from a lot of people, a manager is not most effective when telling everyone what to do. When you're responsible for creative professionals, the best results come from creating the environment, structure, and process in which those people can flourish, and then trying to stay out of the way and remove obstacles.

Michael Lopp (aka Rands, of the influential technology blog "Rands in Repose") captures this concept perfectly in his excellent book, *Managing Humans*[1]:

> *Another favorite move of the busy manager is to schedule a 1:1 for 15 minutes or less. It's the best I can do, Rands. I've got 15 people working for me. First, those 15 people don't work for you; you work for them. Think of it like this: if those 15 people left, just left the building tomorrow, how much work would actually get done? Second, if you've got 15 people working for you, you're not their manager, you're just the guy who grins uncomfortably as you infrequently fly by the office, ask how it's going, and then don't actually listen to the answer.*

You're trying to build a team of people you can trust to do great work, which is why recruiting and hiring are so critically important. To achieve scale and speed in your organization, you simply must hire people you can trust, and then give them as much autonomy as possible.

These people don't work for you; you work for them.

Your Time Is Less Important Than Theirs

A good manager is obsessed with removing obstacles and time-sinks. In many cases, this means taking on tasks that would ordinarily distract people on your team.

To fully embrace this mission, you should adopt the attitude that your time is less valuable than the team's. Although not strictly true in all cases, this philosophy will give you a useful perspective on how to best spend your time.

The typical workday of a manager is different from an engineer's in a few important ways. First, it's full of interruptions and context shifts. Whenever someone has a problem, you're there to help, no matter what you were already doing. Second, a manager usually talks to more people, more frequently, than an engineer. The job is largely about communication. Finally, a manager is a pressure release valve for issues building inside a team. By coming to you first, people can head off more destructive outcomes that interrupt the workflow of the larger team.

These differences make a manager better suited for handling a lot of tasks that affect a team. By spending a few minutes resolving a personal conflict or bureaucratic process question, you can save an engineer hours of interruptions, learning about things in which they have no interest, and dealing with frustration.

---

[1] Lopp, Michael. *Managing Humans: Biting and Humorous Tales of a Software Engineering Manager.* New York: Apress, 2012. 40.

Perhaps it's not totally accurate to say that your time is "less valuable" than your team's, but that the time you invest in certain tasks is returned many times over in what it saves your team.

Example: Hiring

As Course Hero's Engineering and Design team has grown past 25 people, one thing that hasn't changed is that I, the VP of Engineering and Design, still screen all resumes and conduct our first-round phone screens. Although it's appealing at times to farm out these tasks, and I know our senior staff would pitch in without complaint, I continue to resist the temptation.

Screening resumes is arduous, unending work. As soon as you finish one batch, more come in, and unless you're motivated above all else by the excitement of meeting new people and hopefully bringing them into your team, it will wear you down. I love building a team, and even I get fatigued by the process from time to time.

Asking for help starts innocently, but before long could create a burden that's stealing hours a week, taking your best engineers away from the work they love, and sowing seeds of frustration. For these reasons, I plan to continue handling the front end of the hiring funnel for as long as possible.

You Care About Helping People with Their Careers

Career development is one of the most important functions of a manager. Creative, thoughtful people want to make progress, learn new things, and work toward goals, and it's your job to help them. Furthermore, not everyone knows exactly what they want or where they're going, and you need to help them chart that course as well.

Being effective with career development requires many skills. Chief among them are: Being a thoughtful listener; possessing and being able to discuss relevant experience; and attentiveness to peoples' goals and potential opportunities.

Listening

You absolutely must be a good listener—to have the patience to hear and discuss a person's goals and thoughts and give them the consideration required to be useful. Don't interrupt and don't start giving advice until you're confident you've gotten to the bottom of an issue.

If you quickly tire of hearing what other people want or need, management may not be for you.

Experience

It's difficult to advise others on their careers if you don't share their experience. How can you properly advise them on important choices if you've never faced similar ones? Your own path from engineer to manager or leader is a critical teaching point, and you must be comfortable using your experience to educate and advise others.

Furthermore, your credibility as a mentor will be limited if your employees don't trust that you have the proper experience to guide them. Sharing relevant stories and information from your career is an important way to build the confidence of your team in your abilities as a coach.

Attentiveness

Understanding a person's goals is only the first step. Next, you must find opportunities for them to make progress toward those goals. Do you have an engineer who's been aching for a chance to move into mobile development? Remember that the next time you have a position open on your mobile team. Has someone been hoping to add front-end skills? Suggest an upcoming conference or workshop that would help.

Being a manager means constantly trying to match people with the correct opportunities and projects. You'll never make perfect choices, but in order to make the best ones possible, you must remain attentive and mindful of your people at all times.

If you're only able to talk about career growth, but never able to follow through on it, you'll eventually lose your team's faith. Career development isn't just a discussion of an abstract set of goals—it's the realization of those goals through real-world projects and responsibilities.

You're Not Afraid to Correct Behavior

When you see something being done the wrong way, or people behaving inappropriately, are you comfortable being the one to step in? Or would you prefer to wait and hope the issue resolves itself, or that someone else takes care of it?

As a manager, it's your responsibility to handle problem situations. You shouldn't be looking for confrontations, but neither should you run from them. Your team is counting on you to know when and how to correct incorrect behavior.

You need to do the dirty work.

Although you may have to deal with difficult tasks in the short-term, such as coaching an employee through an improvement plan, terminating a poor performer, or conducting a layoff, you should see clearly that these actions benefit the team and company as a whole. If you can't convince yourself of that fact, then either you're not suited for management, or the plan itself is flawed.

These sorts of tasks should be painful. If you actually enjoy firing people, you're probably also not suited for management. You're dealing with real people and significant consequences—it should be difficult to deliver harsh feedback or tell someone their job is gone. Only the conviction that your actions are necessary should push you to make these difficult choices.

You Can Trust Others

An effective manager must be able to delegate responsibilities and tasks to others. In some ways, your effectiveness as a manager is the sum (or product) of the actions of your team, so the more you can delegate, the more leverage you get.

As Andy Grove writes in his classic book, *High Output Management*:

> Because managerial time has a hierarchy of values, delegation is an essential aspect of management. The "delegator" and "delegate" must share a common information base and a common set of operational ideas or notions on how to go about solving problems, a requirement that is frequently not met.

Grove continues:

> [B]e sure to know exactly what you're doing, and avoid the charade of insincere delegation, which can produce immense negative managerial leverage.

It takes time to learn when and how to best delegate work, but the first prerequisite is an ability to trust others to do things that you could yourself do. Without this trust, effective (or in Grove's terms, "sincere") delegation is impossible.

One useful approach to delegation is to look for ways to *make yourself redundant*. By creating the ability in others to accomplish your tasks, you free yourself up to work on other, higher-value projects. And by contrast, those who feel threatened by making themselves redundant (because it diminishes perceived job security) are not management material.

It can be a bit uncomfortable to trust others with tasks you can do, especially when you, as their manager, will be judged on the results. Don't give in to the temptation to jump in and handle it directly—rather, trust your training and monitor progress from a distance. Get involved only if you see things going wrong.

Over time, this trust will be rewarded, as you build a team that can handle not only the tasks you used to do, but a variety of others as well.

You Like to Garden

One of the best metaphors for management is gardening.

To grow a garden, you start by preparing the ground and planting seeds, but if that's all you do, your results will be disappointing. A thriving garden requires constant care, attention, and small adjustments.

Just like gardening, effective management requires patience and diligence. Cutting corners rarely works, and the results correlate strongly with the amount of effort put in.

The seeds of your garden are the people you hire. The soil is the team structure, process, and culture you instill. You must regularly water your garden with one-on-ones, discussions of how to improve things, and events that build team relationships. Every day you should be looking for signs of disease, over- or under-watering, or any of the myriad other dangers that can befall your team. And the harvest, when you ship your product, is a time for celebration that your diligence and hard work have paid off.

Just as you can't grow a potato in a week, no matter how badly you want to, you can't rush things as a manager. Short-term sprints are useful when used sparingly, but if you don't want to strip the soil—burn out your team—you'll save them for true emergencies.

You Obsess Over Details

If you miss something important that affects your performance, that's a problem.

If you miss something important that affects someone else, someone for whom you're responsible, that's a *catastrophe*.

The people you manage depend on your ability to represent their interests, further their careers, and, by extension, improve their lives. That's a lot of pressure. If you let them down by making simple errors, you'll quickly lose this trust, and probably feel pretty bad about it too. The best managers double- and triple-check their work, and they learn techniques and tools to help them. These techniques often involve copious use of notebooks, calendars, and various types of productivity software.

You Care About Accomplishments More Than Friendships

In many ways, being a manager is a lonely job.

One of the most difficult parts of being promoted to a manager, from within a team, is accepting that you can no longer be friends with those on the team. Your priorities have shifted, and your primary responsibility is now to get the best results out of your team—not to be buddies.

As a leader, you now represent the company to the people on your team. Your actions reflect the culture, mission, and goals of the company, and your people will see you more as a company representative than as an individual. This loss of identity can be difficult to accept.

In some ways, becoming a manager means losing a lot of friends. No longer can you commiserate with your team about decisions with which you disagree or make jokes at the company's expense. You always have to be "on" in front of your team, showing your best and most professional side. Furthermore, they don't want to hear about your problems. It's hard to empathize with your boss.

Your friends are now the other managers at your level—and there aren't nearly as many.

Personal Experience: First-Time Manager

My first experience as a manager was at local events search startup Zvents (later acquired by eBay), where I was promoted from web developer to manager of the front-end engineering team. Like a lot of first-time managers, I was more confident than I deserved to be. I thought, "I'm smart; how hard can it be?"

Needless to say, I faced a lot of challenges during that time, but one of the biggest changes I had to accept was the relationship change between me and my former colleagues, now my reports.

I had a lot of fun with the other engineers. We worked hard, but also joked around, teased each other, and spent time together outside the office.

We also shared our successes and failures. Shipping big releases was a bonding activity. More importantly, when we found bugs and other problems, we didn't point fingers or try to find someone to blame. Instead, we shared the responsibility of coming up with a solution. When the VP came over to tell us the site was down, we buckled down and fixed it together.

After I became the manager of the team, though, that changed. Now the VP came to tell me, specifically, when there was a problem. Being friends with the other engineers was now secondary to delivering results. I couldn't commiserate about things like company decisions we found silly, since it was now my job to keep morale up and motivation strong. And it was hard to have fun and goof around when I also knew that I would have to judge peoples' performance.

This shift was hammered home for me, conclusively and permanently, when I first had to help the company prepare for a layoff. In some ways, laying off an employee is harder than firing them, because it's less about their performance and more about the company's. It's an admission that the company, and—by extension—you, have let them down in some way by failing to succeed as a team.

Zvents, like many startups, went through some ups and downs. It reached a point where our burn rate was too high and we simply had to bring costs down. My role in the layoff was small, but it left an indelible mark on my management philosophy. I came to realize that my commitment to help people succeed in their careers, and to make our company successful, are more important than friendships, and that I would be letting my people down if I didn't act accordingly.

This experience, and others like it, that I faced while receiving my education in management from the School of Hard Knocks, had me frequently questioning whether management was the right career choice for me. Ultimately I decided that it was, and I have loved my work ever since, but I wasn't totally prepared for the challenges and decisions I would have to face.

Summary

The job of a manager, when done well, is often difficult and lonely. Those best suited for management positions, and who achieve excellent results in the long term, are individuals who genuinely enjoy enabling the accomplishments of others, are willing to speak up in difficult or controversial situations, and have a tireless attention to details and organization. If you're not naturally this type of person, people management may not be the ideal role for you.

A Manager's Most Important Deliverable

Management work, as compared to engineering work, is abstract and challenging to define precisely. In this chapter, we'll discuss the ways in which a manager adds value to an organization and how to assess a manager's performance.

People moving toward management in their careers often develop a sense of unease about their contributions. This is natural.

While it's fairly straightforward to see and understand your output as an individual, a manager's work product is harder to define. Making peace with this ambiguity, and understanding the subtle ways in which you have impact, are critical steps in becoming an effective manager of people. In many ways, what you're delivering—to your team, your manager, and your organization— is *confidence*.

As a software engineer, I always had a good, rewarding feeling seeing my code running in production. I knew that I had helped complete a project or ship a product. The hours I worked translated directly to an equivalent impact on the company. Furthermore, it was pretty clear whether or not I was doing a good job. Meeting deadlines, making customers happy, and keeping our product free of bugs are all relatively easy to measure.

As I started to take on management responsibilities, a new sort of stress crept in. More than just, "Am I doing a good job?" I started to wonder, "How do I know what a good job is?" And, "What exactly am I doing, anyway?"

There's an initial temptation to quell this anxiety by simply continuing to do a lot of work as an individual contributor—to keep doing your old job while you learn the new one. For me, this meant writing and shipping code. For a little while, this makes you feel better, and might seem like a solution. Over time, however, the pressures of doing two jobs simultaneously will break you. I speak from personal experience.

My first stint as a manager, at the local events search startup Zvents (later acquired by eBay), was as a "player-coach." I continued to work as a senior developer while simultaneously assuming the duties of managing the web engineering team. Not only was I recruiting, hiring, and managing a small team of engineers, but I was also writing and shipping production code under tight deadlines.

At first, I thought I was doing fine. We were keeping up with the development schedule, and everyone seemed as happy as they were before. There was more to do, and I was energized by the new role and happy to do it.

Over time, however, I started to make a few more mistakes—mistakes I normally wouldn't have made. Bugs were slipping into my code, I wasn't collaborating as effectively with others, and I certainly wasn't on top of things with my team in the way a manager ought to be. In hindsight, it's a little embarrassing I didn't notice these changes.

I reached the breaking point—I prefer to call it an epiphany—one evening when I fell asleep on the train home and missed my stop. I'm a light sleeper and almost never fall asleep unless it's on purpose, but on this occasion I woke up a half hour later, groggy and confused, 15 miles from where I was supposed to be. It was the first and last time it ever happened. At that point, I knew I had to choose—be an engineer or be a manager. You can't be both at the same time.

Confidence

What I now understand, years later, after many lessons learned both the hard way and the easy way, is that the primary deliverable of a manager—the most important thing a manager can produce—is *confidence*.

This means different things for all the people you interact with.

Your team is confident that:

- You have their best interests at heart.
- You give them the timely information and tools they need to succeed.
- You help them grow as people and professionals.
- You protect them and advocate for them, insulating them from the distractions of corporate politics.

Your manager is confident that:

- You get good results from your team.
- Your team acts and behaves consistently with company goals and practices.
- Your team is happy and satisfied with their situation.
- You provide adequate career development for the people on your team.

Everyone else in the company with whom you interact is confident that:

- You're doing the things that the company needs you to do, and you're doing them well.
- You're a valuable person to have in the company.

Recognizing that your deliverable is confidence makes some things easier—In particular, determining how much value you're adding. Are these statements true, for your team, manager, and colleagues? If you think they are, how sure are you?

Testing for Confidence

Understanding your effectiveness in delivering confidence is critical.

As an engineer, you typically write unit tests to make sure your code is functioning as desired, and to detect when it breaks. Think about the equivalent for assertions about confidence. Your tests aren't in code, but people. Who can you trust to tell you when people are concerned about a decision you make? What communication patterns can you establish to tip you off to a looming crisis of confidence? Regular one-on-one and staff meetings, if conducted correctly, are an important part of the solution.

Honesty is absolutely essential for you to maintain an accurate picture of your reputation in the company. In your one-on-ones with your team, you need them to be open about any and all concerns they have, to alert you to problems while they're small and manageable. Here some important ways to foster honesty and openness:

- Don't judge ideas when you first hear them.
- Listen and encourage sharing.
- Be honest yourself and open up about important topics.
- Remember details from previous discussions, to show that you take them seriously.

The same is true for team meetings, especially those with senior or more trusted staff. Your internal leaders should be your early warning system—they have the experience to detect issues before others and the willingness to inform you about them. Staff meetings are particularly useful because one or more of your staff may have an inkling or partial indication of a problem, which, combined with the perspectives of the rest of your staff, forms a more complete picture. Again, honesty in your team is critical for your effectiveness. You need as much information as possible.

Warning Signs of Losing the Confidence of Others

Other than unexpectedly falling asleep on a commuter train, how will you know if things are going off track—if you're losing the confidence of others? Here are some warning signs that merit at least further investigation.

People Try to Solve Problems Without You

As much as it may be frustrating to hear about and deal with problems all the time, it's much better than the alternative—that people are trying to handle them without your knowledge. As a manager, you're the chief problem-solver for your team. If you're not accomplishing that, and your colleagues don't believe you can do it, you have a serious problem.

When there's a major bug, service outage, or customer complaint, are you the first person to be notified? If someone on your team is facing a crisis, do they come to you first for help?

People should see you as an indispensable ally for solving tough problems.

People Go Around You

Similarly, it's a sign of trouble when people cut you out of the communication chain. For example:

- One of your reports goes directly to your manager for assistance.

- Your own manager (possibly an executive) prefers to contact people on your team directly.

- People in other parts of the company go directly to your team with questions or requests, skipping you.

In each of these cases, people have lost confidence in your ability to help them accomplish their work.

People Complain a Lot

If you start to hear an increase in complaints from, or about, your team, something's wrong. People who have confidence in you would come to you in a more open and constructive fashion. When they resort to complaining as a tactic, they're skeptical that things will improve and are voicing this frustration.

People Stop Seeking You Out for Help

Successful teams are built of people who help each other, and the sign of a healthy organization is that these requests flow freely throughout. If people rarely ask for your assistance, guidance, or opinion, there's a good chance you've lost their confidence.

Your Perception Doesn't Square with Others

Things happen quickly and there are tons of factors affecting your business, so you may perceive things differently than others from time to time. If you find, however, that you frequently misunderstand important information, such as company strategies, upcoming initiatives, or success metrics, it may be a sign of bigger problem. If your perception isn't consistent with others, or with the company in general, it may be that people aren't making the effort to keep you in the loop.

Dig into the issues and figure out what's causing the discrepancy. Don't accept this kind of inconsistency.

Your Manager Tells You

Finally, your manager might tell you directly about this issue. Obviously, this a serious situation, and you should consider taking whatever steps your manager recommends to remedy it.

Summary: The Value of Confidence

Getting great results from a team requires confidence. Without confidence, people will regress toward second-guessing each other, avoiding risks, and generally not collaborating productively. Confidence underpins morale and enthusiasm for your goals. Building and maintaining confidence in your team, and in others, is an incredibly important and valuable skill, and the most important one for a manager.

Technical vs. Management Tracks: Helping Your People Grow

In the early days of a startup, when there are only a handful of people and every one of those people is consumed with the challenge of finding traction with the product, there isn't much time or need to discuss things like career development. It just doesn't make sense to spend a lot of time talking about such long-term goals when the short-term future of your company is in doubt.

In early 2011, I was part of the founding team of Suitable Technologies, a robotics startup building a totally new type of technology. We called it *remote presence*.

Our first product, a telepresence robot called Beam, was a remotely operated mobile videoconferencing unit. By integrating multiple cameras, an array of microphones, sophisticated Wi-Fi roaming algorithms, a 17-inch screen,

8-hour battery, and a motorized base, we were able to deliver an experience that felt very much like being there in person. The operator of the device enjoyed an immersive experience in a far-off location, with full freedom of movement and communication, and the people local to the device had a much more authentic interaction with the operator—far better than existing, stationary videoconferencing solutions.

For the first 18 months of the company's life, our small team was dedicated to shipping the first version of our product. Nothing else mattered. We all knew that unless we were able to demonstrate some viability in the marketplace, there probably wasn't much of a future or opportunity to build the next version.

Once your company reaches a certain size or stability, however, topics like career development become relevant and important. This development is typically a good sign for your company; it means that people see a true possibility of the company lasting for a long time, and having the opportunity to grow with the team.

It's hard to say exactly when and how this shift will occur. Basically, an increase in the importance of career development in your company correlates positively with a corresponding increase in the chances of the company's long-term success. When risk is high, career development remains an afterthought.

Growth Paths for Engineers

A common mistake, made by companies everywhere, is to reward top engineers by promoting them into management positions. Though this may seem like an appropriate reward for your most productive people, it often backfires, for a variety of reasons:

- Great engineers love writing code. Changing their job in a way that takes them away from writing code may ultimately decrease their happiness with their work.

- Once you've turned an engineer into a manager, it may be difficult to move them back to an individual engineering role without it feeling like a failure. This transition can be made successfully, but often is not.

- Management is hard. Unless someone is truly committed to training themselves on the skills required and building up years of experience, they probably won't be highly effective.

The risk, therefore, is that you take a productive, happy engineer and unwittingly turn them into a mediocre, frustrated manager who feels locked into a dead-end position. This characterization may sound extreme, but all too often it ends in people leaving a company to find a fresh start.

Why does this mistake get repeated so often? Promoting an individual contributor to a management position is the way many careers advance. For technical roles, however, it may not be the best choice.

Furthermore, engineers (especially the good ones) take pride in their ability to solve hard problems, so many of them will see management, if offered, as an interesting challenge to attack. Only after months or years of frustration will they learn that it's not a job they enjoy.

Thankfully, other options exist. Course Hero, like an increasing number of companies, offers engineers two distinct growth paths:

- Technical leadership
- Managerial leadership

Many companies recognize these paths with parallel tracks for advancement. Technical leaders set the examples and standards for professional work in engineering, whereas managers build responsibilities in maintaining the performance, morale, and growth of their teams. Both are necessary functions, and both become more highly valued as a person advances.

Many engineers may not want to be managers, but they absolutely care about career growth. Engineers want to build on their accomplishments, develop a larger role in making their team and company successful, and become leaders in their own ways.

Figure 12-1 captures some of the similarities and differences of technical and managerial career paths.

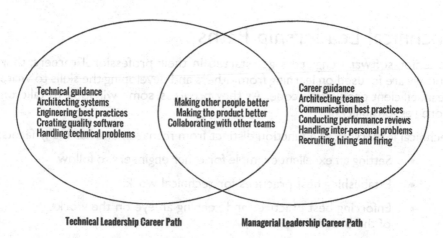

Technical guidance
Architecting systems
Engineering best practices
Creating quality software
Handling technical problems

Making other people better
Making the product better
Collaborating with other teams

Career guidance
Architecting teams
Communication best practices
Conducting performance reviews
Handling inter-personal problems
Recruiting, hiring and firing

Technical Leadership Career Path   Managerial Leadership Career Path

Figure 12-1. Technical and managerial leadership career paths

In a small to medium-sized technology company, it can be useful to illustrate the progression of each career path by example. In most cases, the technical path leads ultimately to chief technical officer (CTO). A startup CTO is the most senior and respected engineer at the company, with a broad understanding of all development activity, insight into the future of the team's architecture and technical needs, and the ability to lead the company's most important engineering projects.

The managerial path, by contrast, typically leads to vice president (VP) of engineering. A startup VP of engineering is usually the manager of most, if not all, engineers in the company, either directly or indirectly. In addition to managing people for top performance and retention, a VP of engineering's top task is often recruiting and hiring talented engineers as quickly as possible, while also building a productive and sustainable engineering culture for the company.

The CTO and VP of engineering roles are complementary in many ways. By focusing on the unique aspects of each, the leaders in these positions can work together effectively to lead all aspects of technical development in a growing company.

In advising engineers on my teams about what career path might be best, and therefore what kinds of skills to develop, I've found it helpful to point to specific individuals as examples. For example, I might ask, "In a few years, do you think you'd like to have a job like mine? Or maybe something more like our CTO?" By discussing the differences in responsibilities between these positions, we're able to start charting a course for a person to make progress in the way they find most compelling.

Technical Leadership Paths

As junior software engineers get started in their professional careers, they typically are focused on learning from others and developing the skills to write clean, efficient production code. As they progress, some will look to take on more responsibility.

Technical leadership, as a function distinct from management, has many facets:

- Setting an excellent example for other engineers to follow.
- Establishing best practices for technical work.
- Enforcing best practices and keeping an eye on the work of the broader team.
- Mentoring other engineers, in an individual or group setting.

- Anticipating future technical needs of the product and company. Researching and crafting potential solutions for those future needs.

- Creating a strong relationship with other parts of the company. Ensuring communication is smooth and effective, both inside and outside engineering.

When speaking to members of my team, I sometimes summarize technical leadership as "making other engineers better."

This type of technical leadership is the growth most engineers prefer—not becoming a manager. They enjoy the technical challenges of their profession and don't want to leave them behind. Ambitious, successful engineers seek bigger and more impactful technical challenges, leading them to leadership positions.

At Course Hero, the first step on the path of technical leadership is to become a lead engineer in one of our product teams. This role of leading a small group of (typically three to five) engineers boils down to two primary responsibilities:

- Set a great example for the other engineers to emulate.

- Make the other engineers better, happier, and more productive.

More specifically, we look for lead engineers to provide mentorship and guidance on all technical matters, to help define engineering best practices, and to ensure that these best practices are being followed in the team. Lead engineers should be thinking a few steps ahead about the technical challenges facing the team, preparing other engineers for upcoming projects or new initiatives.

We also expect lead engineers to be a strong ally for the team's product manager. Together, the lead engineer and product manager work to scope long-term projects, prioritize tasks, and make sure the team has the information necessary to be successful. We look for all team members to contribute product ideas and business innovation, especially the leads.

One of the most important relationships we build at Course Hero is the one between the lead engineers. Together, this group discusses and plans for all the important technical challenges faced throughout the company. In regular meetings, the leads share experiences from their own team about what is working and what isn't, ask for advice from other leads, and generally make sure we're all on the same page about our top priorities, workflow, and culture.

Each lead engineer is responsible for taking this information about best practices, workflow, and tools back to their own team. They instruct their team on how to follow best practices, make use of new tools, and generally understand the guidance of the group of leads. In this way, we've avoided building a reliance on documentation, specs, long meetings, and other techniques that feel heavy-handed or bureaucratic, but have traditionally been needed to manage the organizational complexity of a growing team.

The independence and autonomy of our product teams is a defining characteristic of Course Hero culture, and the lead engineers play a critical role in making this possible.

Managerial Leadership Paths

The other primary path for career advancement in engineering is to become a manager of people. The management path seems to be more widely discussed and understood, which is probably because it's similar to many other professions.

An engineering manager still needs to be technical and have strong technical skills and intuition. Without these skills, a manager will have a difficult time earning the trust and credibility of their team, no matter how big or small. I believe it's useful for a manager to periodically test themselves on their ability to do front-line engineering work for their company, such as writing code that follows established standards, conducting code reviews, performing data analysis, and even pushing fully tested code into production.

Becoming a manager does, however, move an engineer into a less technical role, which is something that many engineers prefer not to do. The primary responsibilities of an engineering manager are no longer related to writing code, but rather finding and solving people-related problems, both now and in the future. Technical skill is critical for being able to do this effectively, but it's no longer the main focus.

Countless books have been written on management itself, so I'll just provide a quick list of the top responsibilities of an engineering manager:

- Recruiting and hiring great engineers
- Providing career advice and guidance for engineers
- Finding ways to deliver high productivity from a team
- Building a culture that encourages excellent work and high job satisfaction
- Detecting and resolving performance and interpersonal problems

As a manager's team grows larger, these responsibilities gradually replace technical contributions.

Engineering managers at Course Hero are distinct from lead engineers. Managers are responsible for the people management functions for a group of engineers across multiple product teams. The roles of managers and leads are quite orthogonal. In fact, it's entirely possible for a lead engineer to report to a manager, who is in turn part of a different team, following the technical direction of another lead engineer.

Combining Technical and Managerial Leadership

It's possible for one person to progress toward both technical and managerial leadership. However, such people are rare (and should be treasured!) and are much more of the exception than the rule. These people have executive potential and bright futures.

One common mistake to avoid, though, is to expect a manager to continue contributing as an individual engineer. Being an effective manager is a full-time occupation. Attempting to be successful as both a manager and an engineer, simultaneously, is truly an effort to hold two full-time jobs at once.

I speak on this topic from personal experience. In my first stint as a manager at Zvents, I thought I could continue to hit my engineering deadlines and throughput goals while also learning the ropes as a new manager, as did the company. Certainly, some hubris was involved. After a few mistake-filled months, I came to the inescapable conclusion that I could probably be a good engineer and a good manager—but not at the same time.

As engineers try to map out their future, I encourage them to focus on choosing a leadership path—technical or managerial—and see where it goes. Even if you're interested in both aspects of engineering leadership, it's best to concentrate on learning these skills separately, so you can acquire and understand the important nuances and details required to be successful.

Transitioning New Leaders

It's best to transition people gradually into new roles, especially when they're as important and difficult as first-time leadership positions. It's unnecessarily risky to thrust an engineer into any kind of leadership without some training, mentorship, or at least a bit of warning about what to expect.

Before starting any kind of transition, it's also useful to share as much advice and experience as possible with your potential leader, so they know what to expect and can make sound decisions about their future. Here is some particularly useful advice to give in this situation:

- This is a new role. This isn't your old job plus a new one at the same time.

- Our expectations of you are going to change. You were chosen for leadership because we think you have the potential for even greater impact by working with others, so that's what we'll expect.

- Please let me know if you start to suspect this role isn't right for you. There's no harm in moving back to your previous responsibilities, and it's far preferable to do that than to remain unhappy and frustrated in the leadership position.

- Continue setting a model example for other engineers. Now that you're a leader, your team will naturally look to you for an indication of how to act and work.

Once you've had some earnest conversations about what to expect, and reached agreement that this is a good opportunity for your employee, yourself, and the company as a whole, it's important to develop a plan. It's not as simple as flipping a switch from engineer to manager or lead engineer. Sometimes external events will force your hand, but whenever possible, it's best to gradually build new responsibilities, with several checkpoints along the way.

Here's a very high-level plan for transitioning engineers into new leadership positions:

- Start with a partial set of the total responsibilities you plan to give someone. For example, with new managers, I first ask them to conduct regular one-on-one meetings with all engineers. These meetings are a simple, easy-to-understand, and relatively low-risk function of management, and also help develop a good relationship between the new manager and their team. Finally, it's a small first test of whether the manager enjoys the work and finds it a productive use of time.

- Continue gradually adding more responsibilities. Each time you do, have an open conversation with the individual about whether they would like to continue the progression toward leadership.

- Have an end date in mind. By this date, the transition should be complete. It's important that the process not seem indefinite or undefined. Like any engineering project, you should track your progress and assess problems as they arise.

Summary

I've found, through years of conversations with thoughtful engineers, that most people are interested in career development, but often don't have a clear idea of what's possible or best for them. The high-level distinction between technical and managerial leadership is a great starting point for many engineers, and can help shape productive careers. As always, the right decision in any situation depends on specific and complex factors. There's no substitute for truly getting to know the people on your team and thinking about what's right for them, and you.

Tricks of the Trade for Engineering Managers

Managers in all disciplines face a wide variety of unpredictable and complex challenges. Compared to a role as an individual contributor, each day tends to be, to borrow a computing term, more *interrupt-driven*—you need to be ready for anything. This chapter contains an assortment of tips, tricks, and advice for many of the situations likely to be encountered by technical managers and leaders.

What Does a Vice President of Engineering Do All Day?

Earlier in my career, I used to wonder what a VP of engineering actually does. I think it's a fair question for people who have never held that kind of role. I would see VPs and other senior staff sitting in a lot of meetings, talking on the phone, and doing a bunch of other things that seemed less productive than writing code. What did they do what was so important? Also, what had they done to deserve that position?

Years later, out of the blue, a member of my team innocently asked me what I do all day. Now that I had become a VP, I could understand and empathize with his question. He didn't mean it in a suspicious way; he was just curious. I realized he truly didn't know how I spent my time, and that we could both benefit by understanding each other's roles better.

Therefore, in response to an honest question, I was motivated to write an honest answer.

But first, some details about the team I lead at Course Hero, for context:

- We have 24 full-stack web and mobile developers.

- Total company size is around 75 people.

- Developers are divided among five (Scrum-like) product teams, each of which has its own product manager and designer.

- We have new developers coming on board all the time, and are always looking for more.

Overall, most of my activities fall into one of two categories:

1. Recruiting and hiring

2. Looking for ways for our team to perform better, now and in the future

And even those two functions are similar in that they're really about helping other people with their own work. My day is more interrupt-driven than a typical engineer's—I know, I used to be one, for many years. Several things can happen, at any time, that will make me stop what I'm doing and shift my focus. For example:

- A new candidate shows interest through our recruiting channels.

- I get new information about an in-process candidate.

- A site performance issue occurs.

- A new bug is reported.

- Someone comes to me with a personal problem.

- Someone comes to me with a problem about our team or company.

- I detect a problem with our team.

Responsiveness is critical for handling these types of issues, so I'm constantly scanning for new ones.

With that background, this is what I do all day. This day, specifically, was Tuesday, May 20, 2014, and a fairly typical one for me:

7:45–7:50 a.m.: Quick e-mail check. Nothing urgent.

8:45–9:30 a.m.: E-mail (and chat) time. Today's topics:

- Check in with our new hires who start next month—what do they need?

- Review all new incoming recruiting opportunities (including 16 new resumes).

- Chat briefly with a team member about details of our web framework.

- Provide feedback to our recruiters about next steps for two candidates from the day before.

9:30–9:40 a.m.: Set up a meeting for the afternoon about a current project that has turned out much longer and more difficult than expected. Determine who needs to be there, the meeting format (Five Whys), and schedule it.

9:40–10 a.m.: Skim a large code review and comments for this project, which is nearing completion. More than looking for bugs, I'm looking to see whether we're consistent in our conventions and patterns, whether I agree with our choices, and whether other team members are doing the same analysis.

10–10:30 a.m.: Phone-screen a new candidate.

10:30–11 a.m.: Eavesdrop on product team stand-up meetings while continuing to review code.

11–11:30 a.m.: Continue code review, asking questions of team members along the way.

11:30 a.m.–12 p.m.: Regular (biweekly) one-on-one meeting with a team member.

12–12:20 p.m.: Go for a walk around the campus. Enjoy the sunshine and weather.

12:20–12:50 p.m.: Lunch (casual, not a meeting) with a team member.

12:55–1 p.m.: Meeting prep. Prepare the notes template, get the room set up, have all material ready to go at 1 p.m. sharp.

1–2 p.m.: Lead the full-team discussion about our troubled project.

2–2:20 p.m.: Synthesize meeting notes to generate specific recommendations for improvement in future projects and circulate with the team.

2:20–2:30 p.m.: Look at a new code review, on a project to start a migration to a new web framework. Try to understand the differences (and improvements) over our current system.

2:30–3:30 p.m.: Do a final review of all peer feedback and notes for an upcoming team member performance review. Write up the review (overall assessment, strengths, opportunities for improvement, and goals), review our budget and finalize a decision on a raise for this person, and share with our CEO and director of people operations for review.

3:30–3:45 p.m.: Phone call with recruiting staff at University of Waterloo to clarify some details of their co-op program.

3:45–4 p.m.: Read Hacker News.

4–5 p.m.: Review new internal (such as marketing and support) projects with our COO and CTO to assess priority and discuss which teams could take them on. Discuss some of the challenges faced by these new teams, and what we can do to improve. Also discuss the best way to bring our new hires onto the teams and generally learn how things are done.

5–5:10 p.m.: Check in on the status of the code review and bug list for the large project.

5:10–5:20 p.m.: Final review of e-mail and new recruiting candidates, mostly intern or co-op possibilities.

8:30–9 p.m.: Review the latest version of our new company recruiting videos and provide feedback.

9–9:10 p.m.: Review details of a new candidate forwarded by one of our recruiters.

10–10:20 p.m.: Chat with a former colleague in an effort to determine whether he's interested in a position.

Not every day is the same, but this one seems pretty typical. It's a great job and I love it, mostly because of all the ways I get to work with and help other people build great software.

Levels of Engineer Performance

I've conducted many performance reviews over the years, and the engineers involved have ranged from difficult and underperforming to superlative and delightful. No matter how well someone is doing, they always want to know how to do better—particularly when it comes to compensation, promotions, and overall responsibility.

Through these years, I've created and refined a simple model for evaluating engineer performance. It has four levels:

- A *mediocre* engineer does what is asked.

- A *good* engineer does what is asked, and does it well.

- A *great* engineer does what is asked, looks for possible problems, edge cases, and overlooked issues, and solves those as well.

- An *outstanding* engineer does all of the above, but also tells you about problems you didn't even know existed, and plans for situations you never envisioned.

To make it even simpler: How much can you improve the happiness and productivity of other people?

The most basic required skill for a software engineer is the ability to write code that meets requirements, is relatively bug-free, and relatively on time. To progress beyond a limited individual role, however, an engineer needs to learn to how to make things better for others.

By *others*, we might mean other engineers, who benefit from suggested improvements for their own code, learning about new techniques, or the enjoyment of working with a pleasant colleague. As an engineer, helping your colleagues fix bugs or solve difficult problems is always appreciated. Even better, help them find the bugs and problems, explain how you did so, and then help with the solution.

An engineer can also improve the productivity of nonengineering colleagues, such as product managers, designers, and testers. Even if they're not writing code, you can still help them with whatever challenges they confront, such as designing new features, brainstorming future projects, or debugging part of a product. You might also build tools to help make them more effective.

Finally, a great engineer should push people in management and leadership to be better. These engineers bring not only ideas and concerns, but also suggestions and solutions. They constructively challenge their managers and others in positions of authority, helping improve the overall organization.

This model of engineer performance is a useful teaching tool. It helps explain what is required to be a successful engineer, and outlines what it takes to advance in an engineering career.

A Word About Promotions

I frequently encounter a misconception about how promotions are given. (Full disclosure: I first encountered this misconception in myself.)

People often overestimate the amount to which their company is observing their performance and assessing their potential. They believe that at some point, their manager will approach them about being promoted into a larger role, based on their ability to grow into that role.

In truth, promotions are usually given to people who are *already* fulfilling the duties of that larger role, and haven't yet been recognized formally for doing so. The promotion is more of a reflection of reality.

If you're interested in a promotion—and not everyone should be, as your current job may be the one you enjoy the most—the best strategy is to look for ways to start doing the job. It's critical to do this in a constructive and helpful way, of course. Don't try to steal responsibilities or decisions from others. Prove that your team, and the company as a whole, will be better off if you're in that new role, and that you're totally capable of being successful. By doing so, you make the decision to give you that role a no-brainer.

Upside-down Engineering Management

Managers, by definition, are caught in the middle—reporting to the senior management or executives above, and responsible for directing the contributors (or other managers) below. Conventional wisdom suggests that the former are more important than the latter. They pay your salary, evaluate your performance, and generally tell you what you should be doing.

It's actually the other way around.

When tech companies hire managers, it's almost always with growth in mind. They're looking for someone who can attract and retain top talent. Strange as it may sound, actual "management" is only a secondary concern.

Therefore, the best way to be successful as a manager, in the long term, is for people to love working for you. You will get amazing results. These results might not be exactly what the people above you asked for, but that's where your skill is required—show that it's better and that they can trust you and your team more than they thought.

Your career is an opportunity to build a group of people who will follow you anywhere, thus making you very valuable yourself. Getting people to love working for you, while still making senior decision-makers happy, is a nontrivial skill that requires a lot of study and practice. (You'll make mistakes.)

Here are some ways to earn the loyalty and trust of your team.

Let People on Your Team Grow

Talented people love to try new things. They're constantly looking to learn new skills, improve their current abilities, and generally expand their knowledge. This is a wonderful characteristic to nurture and encourage in your team.

Here are some examples of how to let technical people grow:

- Let an engineer try a new language or platform for their next project. Do they need to write a message queue and have always wanted to learn more about Erlang? Maybe this is the perfect time.

- Ask a developer to design a new feature themselves, rather than being handed a spec. Put them through the design review process to build an appreciation of what other team members contribute.

- Put your staff in direct contact with customers. Trust them to represent the company's interests and contribute to the requirements-gathering process.

Different things will appeal to different people, but everyone wants to learn.

Grow Yourself

Be humble, and ask your team how you could do your job better. This requires an open, trusting relationship, so do everything you can to nurture that as well. If people trust you, they will not see this as an opportunity to take advantage of you. They will respect you for trying to improve.

You should also apply the same advice and encouragement you share with your team to yourself. Do you encourage people to read technical or business books as a way of developing new skills? Share your own learning from books as you read them. Are you looking for engineers to contribute to open source projects or attend technical conferences? Find a way to participate yourself. Lead by example, demonstrating your own desire to grow, and your team will follow suit.

Fight for Your Team

Show that you advocate their interests throughout the company, whether it's in terms of compensation, strategy, or culture. As a manager, you hold a critical and highly influential role in people's careers. Demonstrate to those people that they can trust you to represent what's important to them and their colleagues.

In my early days as a manager at Zvents, I began to perceive frustration on the part of several engineers at the way product requirements were delivered, which was typically in the form of a long, detailed spec document.

The product managers meant well. They were attempting to provide all the relevant information and instructions in a nicely packaged format, so that it would be clear what needed to be done. From the engineers' perspective, however, this approach had a few problems:

- No matter how detailed a spec was, some things were always missing. This is simply a fact of life in a dynamic, fast-paced environment. Having the spec in hand, however, created an expectation that an engineer should exhaustively process and understand it all before raising any questions, which added a lot of time and effort to handle small clarifications.

- The spec was created with a finality that removed opportunities for engineers to be creative and add their own ideas to the design. Engineers don't typically look to redesign everything in their own image, but still enjoy being able to be part of the discussion.

- Specs get out-of-date quickly, creating a burden on the developer to verify the correctness of everything as it's being implemented.

Reflecting these concerns, I began to push for some changes in our product development process. I felt it was necessary to speak up on behalf of the engineering team.

Thankfully, our product managers were supportive of looking for alternatives (they had their own set of frustrations with the process). With the support of other key staff and internal leaders, we began a process of experimentation and training that eventually led the entire company to adopt Scrum methodology. While not perfect, Scrum was a major improvement for everyone involved (not just engineers), in terms of both productivity and job satisfaction.

If you see people suffering, do something about it.

Be Proactive About Rewards

Sadly, some of the largest raises and promotions are given to employees when they threaten to leave. This is, of course, the worst time for such a reward, as it means you already have a crisis on your hands. Don't let it get to that point, as it may already be too late.

Treat your team like the precious resource that they are, and you will be rewarded in the long run. You should feel that your people are compensated fairly, at all times—not just when they bring it up or when problems arise. If you were to try to hire them today, what would you offer? Is it more than they're currently receiving? Get that fixed.

When people start to wonder whether they're fairly compensated, it starts a dangerous series of dominoes—talking to friends about it, maybe talking with a recruiter, interviewing with other companies, considering other offers— each one increasing the chances they might decide to leave.

Don't let the first domino fall. Be proactive about compensation and rewards, so that it never even becomes an issue.

Preventing Big Projects from Becoming Big Headaches

Has this happened to you?

Your team starts out on an interesting project. You know it's a pretty big one, but not *that* big. You should be able to get it done in a few weeks or so, and it's going to be awesome.

Things go smoothly at first. You've got high-level goals, scope estimates, and everyone pretty much knows what they need to be doing.

Fast-forward to your target ship date. Lots of new features have been added, mostly in the last week, bugs are piling up much faster than the team can handle them, and now the question isn't whether you're going to ship late, but rather *by how much*.

How did this happen?

That's an easy question to answer: Life is complicated. Things happen. They always do.

A better, and more difficult, question is this: How can you prevent this from happening next time?

Here are four specific techniques to prevent projects from ballooning out of control.

Break Things Down

Look for ways to break a project down into smaller, discrete pieces—not just conceptually, but operationally. Make sure that all project tasks have been decomposed into subtasks that take no longer than a day or two, and that team members report their progress just as often. Daily stand-up meetings are an excellent tool for sharing status among all members of a small team.

Ship Constantly

Your team is making its way through a large project, which has been nicely broken down into discrete subtasks. You may still be setting yourself up for a big headache at the end, however, unless you're also completing the release to production for each of these subtasks.

A group of many small tasks, each completed successfully but not deployed, can add up to a huge, monolithic changeset, a mega-merge, and a daunting code review. Ship all these pieces as you go. If you do, your development code base will never differ from what's running in production by more than a day or two's worth of work. This relatively small delta is valuable if you unexpectedly need to accelerate your schedule or make other changes.

Use Feature Toggles

The term *feature toggle*, or *gatekeeper*, refers to a software switch built into your code that allows you to activate (or deactivate) it at a desired time. Toggles have many benefits, but the key one for this discussion is that they allow you to ship your code before the whole project is finished. In order to ship your product constantly, you may need a tool to selectively activate new code as it hits production.

Shipping your code one piece at a time usually means you don't want that partially complete code used until the rest is ready. With a toggle in place, you can ship your code incrementally, running each portion through your full set of reviews and tests. Once everything is fully deployed to production, you can then toggle your new feature on with confidence.

You probably don't even need to write the code for your feature toggle. Many options already exist, for a variety of languages, frameworks, and platforms.

Keep Everyone Working on Only This Project

Over time, it becomes more likely that other projects, issues, and demands on people's time will creep in. Try to make sure this project is the only thing on which your team is working, until it's done. The fewer projects that are in progress simultaneously, the more likely each project will be completed on schedule and with good results.

Finally, managing a large project requires vigilance. It's easy, for both you and your team, to lapse back into what's comfortable, easy, or convenient. Watch closely to see whether things are breaking down, and if so, why.

Or to put it another way: Ship early and often.

Managing People with More Experience Than You

My first experience as a manager (at the local-events search startup Zvents) evolved naturally from being a senior member of a web development team. I could speak confidently and authoritatively on most matters affecting the team, and had the necessary experience to mentor and guide the other engineers.

My second management position, however, at robotics startup Suitable Technologies, presented me with a new challenge: for the first time, I was managing engineers with significantly more experience than me.

Though it adds some complexity, managing people with more experience is certainly something that can be done well. Here are some tips:

- Don't deny the reality of the situation. Everyone on your team, including yourself, needs to see you and treat you as a manager. If you have any lingering self-doubt about your position, do your best to move beyond it.

- Don't pretend to have more knowledge or experience than you do, in an effort to maintain authority. Be honest about what you know and what you don't know, and ask for help from your team whenever needed. They'll respect your self-awareness and desire to learn.

- There's a good chance that your senior engineers aren't totally interested in being managers, or else they might already be in that position. If so, they'll be happy to let you do your job, since they don't want to do it, and they know that if you can't, some of that responsibility may fall to them. They should be your strongest supporters.

- It is, however, important to understand whether any of your engineers do believe they should be the manager, and whether they resent you being given the position. The easiest way to find out is simply to ask. If this is the case, you should explain, and ultimately demonstrate, how your managerial skills will help them grow, and prepare them for opportunities in their own future. Pay special attention, though, to see whether they support you more over time.

In general, your approach to management should be the same, regardless of the relative seniority of your team. You're looking to give people the tools, guidance, and environment they need to do great work. Managing experienced engineers is, in some ways, a special opportunity for you to learn even more and expand your own knowledge and skillset.

Leading a Team Without Deep Domain Knowledge

Another new challenge of leading the software team at Suitable Technologies was that, for the first time, I was responsible for technical work that I didn't fully understand. I had years of experience in web development, but now I was leading a team that was building robotics systems and videoconferencing software.

This situation is similar to managing people with more experience, and the approach is basically the same:

- Be humble. Don't pretend to know things you don't, and try to learn as much as you can.

- Focus on providing value with your management skills. Your team will appreciate these contributions, as they care more about the product they're building.

- Provide mentorship and career guidance for your team. This is fairly independent of your technical domain.

It's fun to learn new things. Leading a team outside your field of experience is a unique opportunity to grow as both a manager and a technologist.

Lessons from a Case Study of Engineering Process

As companies grow larger, they are forced to adopt additional layers of process and hierarchy to manage the increasing complexity of projects and relationships. It's just simple combinatorics. The number of pairwise connections in a group of people grows quickly. The math looks like this:

$$C(10, 2) = 45 \text{ (or "10 choose 2")}$$

This equation indicates that for a group of 10 people, there are 45 possible pairs of 2. Notice how the number of combinations accelerates:

$$C(20, 2) = 190$$
$$C(30, 2) = 435$$

When you consider larger groups, it becomes even more alarming:

$$C(30, 3) = 4,060$$

For a company of 30, there are over 4,000 possible groupings of only 3 people. This is where process becomes necessary, in the form of documentation, meetings, specifications, standards, formal best practices, and so on. These techniques, which are necessary to managing the increasing complexity of a growing team, are also what starts to make it feel like a "big company." What one person calls *process*, another person might call *overhead* or *bureaucracy*.

A critical tipping point comes when an organization is sufficiently large that not everyone knows everyone else. British anthropologist Robin Dunbar famously hypothesized that this point (now known as *Dunbar's number*) is around 150 people, based on research comparing primate and human brain sizes.[1] Whenever it happens, reaching this size in an organization requires the adoption of more-formal organizational structures, titles, and communication patterns. Without shared context between employees, it's important to supplement their interaction with additional guidance and information.

Like many startups, Course Hero strives to maintain the agility, dynamism, and rapid iteration of a small startup, even as we grow larger. Our journey isn't yet complete (75 employees at the time of this writing), but we're off to a great start. This section describes some of the tools, architecture, and yes, *process* we use to maintain agility and a "startup feeling" in our product development team.

Product Teams

The core building block of product development at Course Hero is what we call a *product team*. Similar to Scrum, these teams are composed of a product manager, designer, and a few engineers. We believe strongly, as do most practitioners of Scrum, that the ideal team size is around seven people.[2]

Each product team is focused on one specific area of our product. For example, at the time of this writing, we have five teams:

- New Users (all unpaid use of our site)

- Premier Users (all paid use of our site)

- Tutoring and Q&A Products

- Mobile

- Internal Tools and Services

---

[1] R.I.M. Dunbar, "Neocortex Size as a Constraint on Group Size in Primates," *Journal of Human Evolution* 22.6 (1992): pp. 469–493.
[2] George A. Miller, "The Magical Number Seven, Plus or Minus Two: Some Limits on Our Capacity for Processing Information," *Psychological Review* 63.2 (1956): pp. 81–97.

One of the most important aspects of our structure is that each team is given a large amount of independence and autonomy. As much as possible, we want each team to feel like its own seven-person startup (with one critical difference: the teams have secure funding). Each team has its own mission, list of long-term goals, metrics to track, and roadmap of upcoming projects.

The teams share some process—each team has a daily stand-up meeting, weekly status meeting, and a quarterly planning and vision discussion. We also strive for a consistent engineering workflow, which I'll detail in the next section. But other than those things, the teams are free to come up with ideas and solutions that work best for them.

Development Workflow

Each project, in each team, follows a consistent sequence of steps. Table 13-1 lists each step along with the member of the team responsible for it.

Table 13-1. Development Workflow at Course Hero

Project Phase	Phase Owner
Ideation	Product
Requirements	Product
Scope Meeting	Product
Design Ready	Design
Design in Progress	Design
Architecture Review	Developer
Development Ready	Developer
Development in Progress	Developer
Code Review	Developer
Final Testing	Product
Launch	Product

Some steps may be quick, and others may take days or weeks. In all cases, though, each step must be completed, and there must be a person responsible for that step. In addition, some steps may need to be repeated. For example, if a problem is discovered during Code Review or Final Testing, the project might be sent back to Development in Progress as the team works to fix the code.

Here are some more details on each step.

Ideation

The Ideation phase reflects the creation of a new project idea. These ideas can come from a variety of sources, including employees, customers, and research of market trends. We expect all members of a product team to contribute ideas, not just the product manager.

A project in the Ideation phase should have at least the following:

- A clear definition of the concept
- A high-level business goal

Projects should be prioritized in Ideation, and move to the next step only when the product manager has been able to define requirements for them.

Requirements

The goal of this stage is to build a business case for the project. What needs to be built, and what problem does it solve? What is the opportunity, and what is the potential value of that opportunity?

The information for requirements may come from a variety of sources, including these:

- Competitor/market analysis
- Customer feedback and research
- Internal analytics and data
- Team brainstorm sessions
- Other internal company teams
- Technical performance or reliability

The requirements should describe specific use cases or user stories, and expectations of desired outcomes. Beyond listing new features and design elements, these requirements should also include communication and marketing tasks, expectations of customer support, and other rollout plans.

The Requirements phase is complete when we have a summary description of the project, business case, high-level task list, and a test plan—a set of tests that can be run by anyone on the team to verify that the work is complete and correct.

Scope Meeting

This phase is a meeting with everyone who is expected to be involved with this task, including the following:

- Product owner for this task—a team member responsible for driving this task to completion, but not necessarily a product manager

- Technical lead—a developer with appropriate expertise and experience, but not necessarily the one to complete the work

- Design lead for this task—similar to tech lead, but for front-end design

- Anyone else who has a task assigned as part of the project, such as marketing or customer support

The purpose of this meeting is to review the requirements and provide an initial scope.

Course Hero's work estimates take the form of engineer days or designer days—the "real world" number of days required to complete the task, factoring in overhead such as bug fixes, code reviews, meetings, and everything else that isn't writing code or generating designs. These estimates must also be a Fibonacci number: 1, 2, 3, 5, 8, 13, 21, and so on. Ranges and other values are not allowed. (We require such a number to demonstrate that estimates are necessarily less precise as they grow larger.)

Design Ready

A project in this phase is waiting to be assigned to a designer. This phase gives designers visibility into their upcoming tasks, and allows other team members to prepare for future work.

Design in Progress

At Course Hero, design includes not only the preparation of visual assets, but also user research and front-end development in HTML, CSS, and JavaScript. The Design in Progress phase has three subcomponents:

1. Research into user interface and user experience design trends, looking for best practices and patterns

2. Development and iteration of storyboards, wireframes, mocks, and final messaging and content, including any user research on these concepts

3. Front-end coding and final asset production

Design is complete when the front-end code is finished and reviewed by at least one other designer.

Technical Architecture Review

Before beginning development, we need at least two engineers (with appropriate knowledge) to review the proposed implementation.

This phase is complete when at least one other engineer (not the developer ultimately doing the work) reviews and signs off on the proposed solution.

For small tasks, architecture review might take only a minute. For large projects, this phase could require a design meeting with several engineers.

Development Ready

At this point, the project is waiting for technical implementation. When a developer is available to start, they will assign the project to themselves and begin work. Allocation of resources is accomplished by having developers always select the next, most important project from the master prioritized backlog.

Development in Progress

This is the phase in which the coding gets done.

During development, engineers should consider all possible solutions, regularly review progress with their teammates and the product owner, and adhere to company coding conventions and best practices.

We use Git for code version control, and one of our few strict rules is that all new development—no matter how big or small a project is—must be done in a branch (not master). Only after Code Review (the next phase) is complete, may the code be merged back into master.

The engineers on a project are also responsible for creating all necessary unit and functional code tests. We've developed tools to help with this process, such as a client-side precommit Git hook that automatically runs all unit tests on a commit, aborting the commit if any tests fail.

Code Review

When coding is complete for a project, the project's lead developer needs to perform a code review with at least one other developer. We leave it up to the developer to choose the most appropriate reviewer. Typically, this is another developer with good knowledge of the area(s) of code affected.

As described previously, one important rule that we strictly enforce is that no code should be merged back into our master branch without a complete code review.

The Code Review phase is complete when the following are true:

- The code is complete.
- The code review is complete.
- The code has been tested and verified by the developer(s) against the test cases in the initial project description.

Quality Assurance

Course Hero has no full-time testing staff, so all members of the team share the responsibility to test our products.

Projects in this phase are ready to launch but need to be tested, and should be running on one of our staging servers. The testing tasks may be shared, but final sign-off on the readiness of the project is the sole responsibility of the team's product manager.

Launch

We made it! At this point, the work is running live in production.

Course Hero puts every new project through an A/B test to verify that it's an improvement on our existing product. Each test is unique, but we typically measure metrics such as the following:

- Web traffic impact
- Conversion rate
- New user sign-up rate
- Revenue impact
- Bounce rate

If the test results look good, the final step is to optionally execute a communications plan around the new feature or product. For example:

- Notify internal stakeholders or customers
- Update customer support about the feature
- Launch external marketing and communication

The project is totally finished when all communications, test analyses, and bug fixes are complete.

Course Hero's Engineering Principles

The Course Hero product teams have a large amount of autonomy and independence, and are free to solve challenges in whatever way suits them best. To provide high-level consistency for our engineering team, we've established a list of five engineering principles:

- Ship Early and Often
- Only One Project at a Time
- Testing is a First-Class Problem
- Communicate Openly and Frequently
- Always Be Recruiting

Here's a short description of each principle.

Ship Early and Often

A common pitfall of large projects (or even small projects that unexpectedly become large) is that by the time they are complete, the changes are so large that a huge amount of time is expended merging code, testing, and checking initial requirements. Our preferred approach is to break a project into small pieces and ship those pieces to production incrementally. Here are some more specifics of how we do this:

- Engineers conduct code reviews throughout a project, rather than waiting until the end.

- As subtasks are completed, they're code reviewed and merged to our master branch.

- A feature toggle is used to allow partially completed projects to be shipped to production, but remain inactive until the entire project is complete, at which point we can simply "flip the switch" to activate them.

Only One Project at a Time

We try to resist the temptation to do a lot of things at once. Engineers should say no when necessary, or at least, "I'll have to do it later." We believe that an engineer should be focused on one task—whichever one is currently the most important—and give that their full attention and energy until it's fully completed.

Testing Is a First-Class Problem

Testing is an important part of everyone's job. For an engineer, testing your code is just as important as writing it. For a product manager, testing a product before release is just as important as doing market research and writing requirements. Testing should never be shortchanged because of other tasks, and test plans must be completed as part of a project.

In addition, it's important to include the time to develop software tests in all project estimates. Don't leave tests out in hopes that you'll get to them later.

Communicate Openly and Frequently

We believe strongly in the DRY (don't repeat yourself) principle, especially at the team level. Before implementing a new library, component, or widget, ask around to see whether there might already be something similar that could be used.

We encourage all team members to leverage their team to the fullest—to ask for help when they get stuck, or to clarify something that's confusing. A simple question can save hours of work and headaches.

Always Be Recruiting

As a company in constant growth, we want everyone to share a recruiting mindset. You never know where an opportunity might arise, so it's important to be attentive and proactive.

We strive to make every candidate's experience at Course Hero an excellent one. Even the people not directly involved in our recruiting or hiring process should be welcoming and friendly to all visitors they encounter at Course Hero. Every person, not just job candidates, should leave our office thinking, "I really want to work there." Even if we don't end up extending an offer to a candidate, they might share their experience with others.

Finally, having a recruiting mindset means thinking critically about how to make Course Hero the ideal place for you to work. We don't want to settle for what's good enough right now. What will help us attract the best and brightest for the future as well?

Pair Programming

One of the most important ways we try to build a culture of collaboration at Course Hero is through the use of pair programming.

Our definition of *pair programming* is any situation in which two engineers are working on a problem at one computer, and only one of them is controlling the keyboard and mouse. We don't force people to pair but try to encourage it whenever possible. The benefits are numerous:

- Pairing is an effective way for engineers to learn from each other. For this reason, it's typically best to let the less-experienced engineer control the computer. Otherwise, they may have a hard time keeping up.

- Pairing catches a lot of bugs. Having an extra set of eyes on a problem can save a lot of time spotting problems, and working next to another engineer tends to make people more careful too.

- Pairing can be fun. Working on a hard problem can feel less intimidating or frustrating when someone is by your side.

- Pairing is an excellent way to converge on common coding standards and best practices. This kind of informal information sharing is a beneficial side-effect of working on projects together, and the more pairwise combinations you foster in your team, the faster you'll achieve consistency of thought.

Many people are reluctant to try pair programming because they think it will decrease a team's throughput by half. The benefits I've described, however, often outweigh any short-term delay and lead to great productivity improvements in the long run.

Summary

Successful managers have toolboxes with lots of different tools in them. In this chapter, we've discussed a variety of strategies, techniques, and tools to solve some of the myriad challenges you'll face while building and leading a team.

In your experience as a manager, you'll undoubtedly create and archive tips and tricks of your own. Over time, you'll learn to recognize familiar problems and challenges, anticipate likely outcomes, and call on the most appropriate techniques at the correct times. Maintain an open mind and a desire to keep learning throughout your journey.

Career Advice for Software Engineers

Before I became a manager of engineers, I was an engineer. This appendix contains advice on a variety of topics to help software engineers find a great job, fulfilling work, and growth in their careers.

Career Paths: Silicon Valley vs. Traditional Technology Companies

Silicon Valley venture capitalist and Google/YouTube veteran Hunter Walk once posted a tweet that prompted me to more deeply examine something I'd been thinking about for a while—something I wish people had told me when I was starting my career in technology.

> Optimize for working w smart folks early in career. Today hung w peeps i met 2001, 2005, 2007. All doing amazing stuff.[1]

---

[1]Hunter Walk (hunterwalk), 27 Dec 2012, 6:09 p.m. Tweet.

I started my career by working in two big companies, Xerox (at the famous Palo Alto Research Center, or PARC) and Hewlett-Packard (at HP Labs). The career path for a software engineer at a large tech company such as HP, IBM, or Intel typically looks something like this:

- Software engineer
- Senior software engineer
- Staff software engineer
- Senior staff software engineer
- Principal software engineer
- Master software engineer
- Software architect
- Chief software architect
- Fellow
- CTO

Similar progressions exist for other types of engineering as well. Typically, there's a parallel track for management that diverges at some point, and leads to positions such as these:

- Engineering manager
- Senior engineering manager
- Director of software engineering
- Senior director of software engineering
- Vice president of software engineering
- Senior vice president of software engineering
- Executive vice president of software engineering

In both cases, you're "working your way up" (my list is upside down), in the way that people in the United States have thought about career advancement since at least World War II.

After living and working in both worlds, I now understand that the Silicon Valley startup career path looks a little different:

- Company A
- Company B
- Company C

- Company D
- Company E

Here's the key difference: in the traditional path, your career success is defined mostly by your individual advancement. In the Silicon Valley path, however, you may have different positions at each company, depending on what you like to do, but your career success, especially in financial terms, will likely be dominated by the overall success of the companies. Ask any of the first 1,000 employees at Google, no matter what their title. Therefore, it's vitally important for you to work with the people who are most likely to succeed, and maximize the opportunities for doing so. If you work at Company B with an outstanding team, but the concept didn't quite make it, your chances at Company D will be much better if you can work with some of them again.

Furthermore, your opportunities at subsequent companies will come from the people at the previous ones. Otherwise, your fate is in the hands of recruiters and HR departments. If the all-star team from Company B is reassembling for another try, you want them to be thinking of you.

This can also apply to projects—within companies or open source, for example. Even if you're not switching companies, look for projects with great people. I certainly met some at both Xerox PARC and HP Labs, and did end up working with some of them later. I just wish I had known how important that was going to be.

In summary, here are the lessons to share from my experience:

- Do everything you can to work with great people.
- Figure out who's on your team—the people you want to work with again, and build your career with.
- Go where the great people are. (They may not be where you think.)
- If there aren't great people where you are, leave.

How to Find the Best People to Work With: Be One

To build a successful career in Silicon Valley, it's important to find great people to work with. How can you make this happen? A good place to start is to examine that question from the other direction. Namely, "How do I make sure others think I'm one of the best people to work with?" It's a two-way street.

Let's face it. Not everyone may want to work with you. Even if you find the company, group, or project of your dreams, they may not accept you in return. I haven't gotten an offer for every job for which I've interviewed.

So how do you get yourself to the top of the others' lists of *people with whom I'd like to work again?*

Be Good at What You Do

It may seem obvious, but it's worth stating—you should be a strong practitioner of your craft. A mobile app startup doesn't want *an* iOS developer; they want *the best* iOS developer. Companies don't want someone who can perform all the functions listed in their job descriptions; they want someone who can do them all *and then some*.

Keep your skills sharp and current. Don't coast. Just because you can do your current job with the skills you already have, doesn't mean you should. Learn new skills. Try new techniques. Look to do your work better.

Here's a test: are you always asking others for help, or do they come to you?

If you're not the expert, strive to get there. And asking others for help is a great way to start.

Know What You Do

People have different skills, and most teams require a wide variety. Understand where you create the most value—where you can provide the most improvement over the next best alternative.

This may not be as simple as you think. Drawing again on my experience in software, if you describe yourself as, say, a Ruby developer, your ability to write Ruby code is only the beginning. How versatile are you? If your team needed to build something using C++, would you be able to help? What if they needed someone to learn Hadoop for a new project? Would they ask you first? Does your code need much maintenance? Do your colleagues read your code to learn the best way to do things? This topic probably merits an entire post of its own, just for software development.

At this point in my career, I contribute more value as a software manager than as a developer. This obviously means that some opportunities aren't right for me—if good management is already in place, or the team is too small to need it yet, for example. But if you have a growing team that's having a hard time keeping up with the competing demands of product management, reliability, development speed, and overall employee morale, I want to be the one you think of first.

Stay in Touch

This is the easy part. Don't lose contact with the superstars in your life. There are plenty of tools with which to do this—the best choice depends on your contacts. Go where they are, and stay in touch.

How to Get Ahead: Document Everything

If you're looking to advance in your career—to get new opportunities, responsibilities, authority, and, yes, paid more—I have a simple but invaluable piece of advice.

Write down everything you do.

Every day, week, or month, add to a running list of your accomplishments at work. Include as much as you can think of, no matter how big or small.

As much as you might like to think that your manager, peers, and colleagues appreciate and remember all of your wonderful contributions, the fact is that they don't. They have their own busy lives to worry about, their own projects, and their own interests to consider. It's not intentional or antagonistic—they simply don't remember everything. That's why you need to give them a little help.

If your company performs annual reviews, there's probably a part of the review process to go over your accomplishments during that time. You might be asked to provide a list. Coming up with a summary of your accomplishments for the past year is difficult and time-consuming, and you're certain to miss some important things. It's much easier to add to a document, incrementally, throughout the year.

Even if you're not asked for such a list, it will still be valuable. Someone's going to be figuring out what you did, and if you can easily spot omissions, it only makes your overall case stronger.

What if your company doesn't even do regular reviews? (This is a bit of a warning sign about your company, in many cases, but would understandable in early-stage startups.) Well, there's still probably going to come a time when you would like a raise, promotion, or freedom to work on new projects. You're going to be able to make a stronger case for yourself, in any discussion, by having a comprehensive document of your accomplishments handy.

Finally, this list gives you the chance to create a positive impression. In all of the preceding cases, I'll bet that whomever you're speaking with (manager, colleague, interviewer) is unaware of many of the things on your list, which means you're going to surprise them to the upside. You get to overdeliver, which is a great way to get someone feeling good about you.

It doesn't have to be fancy. Open a document in Google Docs, Microsoft Word, or your favorite text editor, and just start typing. You'll be glad you did.

The Most Important Quality for Software Candidates: Teachability

In discussing and preparing for software interviews, people typically focus on the technical aspects: algorithm design, data structure selection, performance and complexity analysis, and so on. As our interview process has evolved and matured at Course Hero, however, the factor that probably rules out more candidates than any other, is this: teachability.

Everyone is going to learn and grow into a new position. Nobody is a perfect fit when you first meet them. The question, therefore is, How much of an investment do we need to make in this person, and how much will it pay off?

Junior candidates will require more mentorship than senior ones, but in both cases, some will be required. Even for people who already are skilled programmers, they need to learn our process, code base, and conventions. In our interview process, we're looking for signs that this mentorship will be productive. It really boils down to two questions:

- Is this person interested in learning?
- Is this person capable of learning?

There are a few ways to demonstrate that you are teachable in an interview setting:

- Receive and incorporate feedback from your interviewer. If they suggest a way to approach a problem, listen. They're not trying to trick you. (If they are, I suggest you interview somewhere else.) Respond to that feedback and try to incorporate it into your work. You might know a better approach, but if you decide to say so, you need to be right.

- Apply things discussed earlier in the interview to subsequent questions or problems. This is a great way to demonstrate that you've learned something.

- Communicate and have an active dialogue as you work through things. Good communication is an indication that people will be able to have productive work sessions with you.

- Talk about projects where you've tried to learn things, beyond strictly what was asked. Show that you're self-motivated to learn, improve, and share knowledge with others.

Presenting yourself as a teachable team member can really set you apart—in your next interview and throughout your career as well. By nature, *being teachable* means that you are receptive to testing and trying new approaches. Your mentors and colleagues will be eager to share their unique perspectives, and you'll learn how to attack projects from a variety of angles. This experience—and your willingness to learn—will be invaluable at your current position and beyond.

The Most Common Mistake in Startup Job Applications

As someone who has managed technical teams for several years, at large and small companies, I've received and read hundreds, maybe thousands, of e-mails from applicants. You certainly learn some heuristics to help identify the good ones quickly, but you also spot frustratingly common mistakes. In my experience, the most common mistake for people applying to startups, the one that has undermined the chances of some otherwise qualified candidates at my company, and certainly others as well, is as follows:

You didn't tell us why you want the job. *This* job.

If you haven't spent any time learning about us and what we need, why should we do the same for you?

Every candidate that gets to the interview stage requires us to do hours of preparation, interviews, and discussion. If your introduction is generic, I'm led to believe that you've contacted dozens of other companies as well. If we're going to invest our time in getting to know you, we'd like to know you're serious about us.

It's different for bigger companies, which have hiring processes that involve more people and put your information through some normalization (a huge hiring database) anyway. But at a startup, every hiring decision is so important that it takes careful consideration.

Here are some specific manifestations of this problem, which you should avoid in your own communications.

Don't:

- Send an introduction or letter that has no information specific to the company or position

- Write "let me know if you have any good opportunities for me"—you should be explaining that to us

- Apply for a position that clearly does not match your background, without any explanation why

By contrast, here's how you can stand out.

Do:

- Tell us why you want this job, specifically
- Demonstrate that you're interested in our company and products
- Explain how you would be able to do the job, to the best of your ability
- Describe examples of past work that would apply

And always include an up-to-date resume. It may seem quaint, but a resume is still one of the most concise, portable summaries of a person's skills and experience you can find.

The Most Common Mistake in Startup Job Interviews

This happens way too often:

Q: "Tell me about this recent project on your resume. What was your role, and what did you contribute?"

A: "Well, we built a tool to…"

Whoa, stop right there.

Any interview response that includes *we* is not useful. We're not interviewing your whole team. We're interviewing you. Tell us what *you* did.

Be egotistical! Be self-obsessed! (But don't lie.)

If you're able to talk only about what *we* did, it unfortunately sounds like you didn't do anything. For example:

Bad: "Our team refactored the order-processing system to improve performance."

Good: "I reimplemented an existing Python library for order processing in C++ and added multithreading to improve performance."

Great! You've just given me a half dozen things to ask about and dive into. The more detail, the better. Don't be too modest—this is your time to show off. Since you're here in our office, you've convinced us you want the job; now convince us you can do it.

Four Ways to Improve Your Next Job Interview

Job interviews can be stressful, confusing experiences. Here are four simple tips to increase your chances for success and enjoyment of the process.

Learn About Your Interviewers

The team interviewing you has almost certainly looked you up on Google, LinkedIn, and probably Facebook and Twitter too. You can do the same. For example, search their company on LinkedIn for the type of role for which you're interviewing. Even if you can't find people specifically, you can get an idea of the culture and skills that are important.

Come with Suggestions

During the interview, show that you're really interested in this opportunity. They're investing time in you, so demonstrate that you've done the same. Show that you've thought about why this job in particular is so important. Show that you've taken the time to research what they do and try to understand it.

One of the best ways to prove your interest is to offer suggestions on how to improve their product, process, or some other part of the company. They may disagree with your idea, but they'll appreciate that you took the time to try.

Don't Call It Resume.pdf

Properly naming a resume file is evidently still a widespread problem. I currently have 14 files called Resume.pdf in my default download folder alone. Put your name and something descriptive in the file name, so it's easier to find and remember.

For example: josh_tyler_resume_sw_engineer.pdf

Five Minutes Early Is Much Better Than Five Minutes Late

Obviously, it's better to be early than late, right? But let me explain some reasons why, that you might not have thought of.

First, it might come across as rude. You're taking this seriously, right?

Second, if you arrive early, your interviewers might not be fully prepared. This gives you a tiny psychological edge.

Finally, if you're late, you're possibly shortening the time available to impress the team with your skills. If you're fortunate, your interviewers will have extra time to run late. But they might not.

Remember, your interviewers have to start by assuming you're not going to get an offer. The interview is your time to prove you should. Don't short-change yourself.

Deep-Link to GitHub: Make Your Resume Stand Out

Many software engineering resumes, cover letters, and job applications now include links to personal repositories on GitHub, the popular code hosting site, which is great. For software developers, this is your portfolio. Unfortunately, though, it's hard to find the important information there—most projects have layers of directories, boilerplate code, and lots of stuff written by other people. It's not useful, for example, to see that you were able to generate the default scaffolding code for a Rails app.

There has to be a better way!

I have a suggestion: deep-link to a few highlights inside your GitHub repo—files or changesets that show off some of your best code or design work. Take the reader right to the good stuff.

To show an example from my own (admittedly sparse, out-of-date) GitHub...

This is OK:

```
https://github.com/jtyler
```

But this is better:

```
https://github.com/jtyler/jquery_coordinates/blob/master/jquery.coordinates.js
```

Choose carefully to show off your best work!

Index

Get the eBook for only $5!

Why limit yourself?

Now you can take the weightless companion with you wherever you go and access your content on your PC, phone, tablet, or reader.

Since you've purchased this print book, we're happy to offer you the eBook in all 3 formats for just $5.

Convenient and fully searchable, the PDF version enables you to easily find and copy code—or perform examples by quickly toggling between instructions and applications. The MOBI format is ideal for your Kindle, while the ePUB can be utilized on a variety of mobile devices.

To learn more, go to www.apress.com/companion or contact support@apress.com.

Other Apress Business Titles You Will Find Useful

From Techie to Boss
Cromar
978-1-4302-5932-9

**How to Recruit and Hire
Great Software Engineers**
McCuller
978-1-4302-4917-7

**Managing Humans,
2nd Edition**
Lopp
978-1-4302-4314-4

**Managing Projects in
the Real World**
McBride
978-1-4302-6511-5

**No Drama Project
Management**
Gerardi
978-1-4302-3990-1

**Preventing Good People
from Doing Bad Things**
Anderson / Mutch
978-1-4302-3921-5

**Technical Support
Essentials**
Sanchez
978-1-4302-2547-8

**How to Secure Your
H-1B Visa**
Bach / Werner
978-1-4302-4728-9

**Tech Job Hunt
Handbook**
Grossman
978-1-4302-4548-3

Available at www.apress.com

Printed in the United States
by Bookmasters

Printed in the United States
By Bookmasters